THUILLIER, R.   Marcus Adams

AS   2/86   17.95

0 906053 56 0

Please renew/return this item by the last date shown.

So that your telephone call is charged at local rate,
please call the numbers as set out below:

	From Area codes 01923 or 0208:	From the rest of Herts:
Renewals:	01923 471373	01438 737373
Enquiries:	01923 471333	01438 737333
Minicom:	01923 471599	01438 737599

L32b

MARCUS ADAMS

Marcus Adams. A portrait taken by his son Gilbert to commemorate his eightieth birthday.

MARCUS ADAMS

Photographer Royal

Rosalind Thuillier

Foreword by Patrick Lichfield

AURUM PRESS

AUTHOR'S NOTE

Marcus Adams's work was exhibited annually throughout his career in all parts of the world. Most of the plates used for this book are those that were exhibited; since it would take another book to catalogue each exhibition, details of these have had to be omitted. Likewise his photographs were published in their thousands in newspapers and journals all over the world and it would require a *catalogue raisonné* of gigantic proportion to list them.

While every effort has been made to identify the sitters, this has proved impossible in the case of many of the unnumbered photographs. However, it was thought that they should not be excluded on these grounds. Similar problems were encountered in dating the photographs, and though approximate dates have been given where possible, some remain undated.

The author would like to apologize to anyone incorrectly attributed.

Some of the titles to the portraits here were those given by Marcus Adams himself when submitting them for exhibition.

The photograph of Marcus Adams on p. 71 is by Joseph McKeown.

All photographs are in the collection of Gilbert Adams unless otherwise stated.

Copyright © Rosalind Thuillier and Gilbert Adams 1985

Published by Aurum Press, 33 Museum Street, London WC1A 1LD

ISBN 0 906053 56 0

Designed by Neil H. Clitheroe

Origination by Culver Graphics Litho, London

Phototypeset by Comproom Ltd, London

Printed in Singapore by Toppan Printing Co. (S) Pte. Ltd

CONTENTS

ACKNOWLEDGEMENTS

Many people contributed enormously during research for this book. My husband, Gilbert Adams, FRPS, kept close supervision on facts, and without his cooperation this book would not have been written. He made available all letters, writings, publications, notebooks, negative books, glass negatives, photographs and related ephemera, together with all copyright material in his collection.

I am indebted to Barbara Thuillier who tirelessly discovered the addresses of nearly seven hundred of Marcus Adams's sitters, and numbered and measured many of the prints. Her efforts were unstinted. Equally I am indebted to Betty Addington for her help with the picture research. This was no easy task as many of the pictures are not numbered, preventing their being matched to sittings recorded in the negative books. She spent an icy cold winter in an old milking parlour sifting through numerous prints attempting to discover who was who between 1900 and 1959.

To Leslie Beck, late of Kodak, and Bertie Bray, late of the *Illustrated London News*, I am indebted for anecdotes. To the late Henry Maule for so generously giving his valuable time and notes on royal sittings after an interview with Gilbert Adams I am profoundly grateful.

With Joan Luke (Farquharson) I spent many happy hours talking over the workings of The Three Studios at 43 Dover Street. Her help as Marcus Adams's printer for thirty years was invaluable to me.

The children of my husband, Anthony Adams and Susan Fyffe, supplied reminiscences of their grandfather.

A number of people sent their own photographs by Marcus Adams, many of which are included in this book; others, for reasons of space, have regretfully had to be excluded.

Many people wrote letters setting out their experiences of being photographed at the studio of Marcus Adams. Among these were Lord Astor, Lord Dalhousie, the late Lord Reading, Mrs Robert Morley, John Buck, Lady Elizabeth Longman and Mrs Vivian Dudley.

There were in addition so many people who agreed to be interviewed, and again I found the time afforded to me invaluable. Although too numerous to mention, they included the Marquess of Bath, the Marchioness of Normanby, Lord Southborough, Lord Dudley, Lord Cadogan, Lord David Cecil, Lord Catto, Barbara Cartland, John Buck and Una Lewis.

Others who helped in various ways include Mrs Manvell, Ann Gutch, Dr Hugh Vaisey, Sydney James Vintner, June Park (Mrs Mardall) and William Thuillier.

The Wiltshire County Library, Marlborough, assisted by producing nearly fifty titles in under one month.

I should like to thank, as ever, Jim Reynolds; my editor, Angela Dyer, for her close cooperation; and the book's designer Neil Clitheroe.

I should like to end by saying that to all those who sat for Marcus Adams I am deeply indebted. Without the twelve thousand subjects there would of course have been no book.

ROSALIND THUILLIER

FOREWORD

Marcus Adams was a perfectionist. Looking at these photographs one realizes very quickly that unless he had been, they could never have been taken.

To us now, in the age of virtually foolproof cameras when almost anyone can take a technically passable photograph, it is hard to appreciate the conditions under which he worked. Imagine that you have to concern yourself with lighting, with focusing, with manoeuvring your subject in front of a carefully arranged and elaborate setting while grappling with twenty feet of rubber tubing on the end of which is the shutter release; imagine that between shots you have to wait while your assistant (hidden in a hole in the wall behind the camera) changes the plates, and that the shutter speed is such that your subject must not move, and then remember that that subject each time was a *child* – surely the most fidgety, perverse and unpredictable of God's creatures – and you will see what I am talking about!

Despite these technical and physical handicaps Marcus Adams succeeded in taking photographs that were artistic, moving and psychologically profound. He managed to capture, as did Julia Margaret Cameron in the nineteenth century and Lord Snowdon in his early work, the unique quality of childhood. His pictures are collectors' pieces.

If Marcus Adams had many things against him in our terms, he was fortunate in one respect: he was able to take advantage of the gap left between the demise of the painted portrait and the arrival of the ubiquitous family snapshot. Parents who wanted a record of their children growing up came regularly to his studio, and among these of course were the Royal Family.

It may seem from looking at this book as if his work was confined to the rich and the privileged, and in some ways this is true. But in one important respect it is not. In that pre-television age it was Marcus Adams's photographs which brought the Royal Family to the people for the first time. His portraits of the little Princesses – at the piano, with their dogs, doing a jigsaw – were daringly informal for their time, and they brought the natural, human side of royalty into the lives of people both rich and poor all over the world.

These photographs will appeal to many different types of people of many ages, and for many reasons. I wholeheartedly recommend them for their charm, their beauty, their technical mastery, and their record of a bygone age.

PATRICK LICHFIELD

I

THE STUDIOS

'To realize these subtle and fleeting expressions one must be fit and in tune to the most sensitive possibilities . . . or you will miss them, as sure as you miss the fleeting tints of a sunset . . . you must be as sensitive as a photographic plate . . . and as quick as a swallow.'

It was fortuitous that Marcus Adams ever became a photographer. On leaving school in Reading in 1890, at the age of fifteen, he joined the Wesleyan Church and became deeply attached to the Methodist religion. By day he worked in a solicitor's office, copying documents for the small remuneration of fifteen shillings a week. The work must have seemed dull to a man who was later to achieve fame and fulfilment by producing the most outstanding, and technically incomparable, child portraits of his time. Towards the end of his life Adams wondered whether he should have concentrated on fine art, for which he trained at Reading Art College and later in Paris. At Reading he learnt the art of using paint and observing tonal values; the latter skill he found able to apply to photography as well as painting.

Being the seventh child of an artistic family may have contributed to his genius. Three of them energetically pursued artistic careers. His eldest brother Christopher was a portrait painter and distinguished miniaturist, a council member of the Royal Miniature Society who exhibited over many years at the Royal Academy, while assisting in the Adams photographic studios in both Reading and London. His sister Lilian was a well-known painter who lived in Paris and exhibited for over fifty years at the Paris Salon.

In 1892 Marcus Adams became apprenticed to his father, Walton Adams, in Reading. Walton Adams's first studio in Southampton had been renowned for its fine, serene portraits of English and European royalty. Walton had been a pioneer photographer in the 1860s when he assisted Dr Maddox on the dry plate process. He then moved to Brixton (it is thought in order to enter the tailoring business), but this change lasted little longer than a year, after which he went to Reading with his wife and seven children. The Blagrave Street photographic studio in Reading became very much a family affair, with Marcus Adams as apprentice, Chris and Marcus cleaning floors and polishing brass plates, and another sister, Elsie, helping with daily production.

During the early part of the century Marcus Adams was gaining valuable experience in all types of photography. He was photographing cabbages and kings simultaneously: when King George V visited Suttons seed factory, Marcus was commissioned to take photographs commemorating the visit. He was also assisting Charles Keyser, the millionaire landowner of Aldermaston Court, whose life's work was Norman architecture, in producing illustrations for many of his books. Often the two would set out together with Henry Taunt of Oxford, another eminent photographer, driven by Jacob, Mr Keyser's chauffeur. Cars in those days had wooden wheels and hard pneumatic tyres, and lighting was by oil and acetylene lamps.

Marcus Adams went about his photography on these occasions in a methodical manner with about five cameras, including the Sanderson outdoor type, and a multiplicity of lenses. The cameras were set to expose for long periods on to various aspects of church architecture. To obviate some very long exposures of large interior scenes, magnesium flash powder was used. This was a highly dangerous process as it had a tendency to explode at the wrong moment. On one occasion a large quantity of smoke went up into a church tower and was seen by a passer-by from the village, who summoned the fire brigade.

During these years at Reading Marcus Adams began to establish a reputation for portrait photography, and with it his confidence increased. He went to Foxhill, the home of Sir Rufus Isaacs – later to become Lord Chief Justice and, later still, Viceroy of India – to do a series of portraits of Sir Rufus. The success of these pictures encouraged Lady Rufus to invite him, on one occasion, to photograph their luncheon visitor. She kept the secret as to who the guest was to be. It was Mr Asquith. So pleased was everyone with the portrait that Lady Rufus played a similar game later on, when the guest turned out to be Mr Lloyd George.

In these early days of photography a great variety of papers was used and a great number of chemicals was required, all of which Marcus Adams became familiar with in the many styles of portraits he was taking, of both children and adults, at that time. No panchromatic materials were available. All the prints were made from orthochromatic coated glass plates. Some prints were toned, which rendered them more permanent. (It is unlikely that contemporary photographs will last in the same manner.) At that period most photographs were made by contact, there being no enlargement processes, and the Adams made their prints in daylight in a large greenhouse. A number of Marcus's mezzotint-style prints, remarkable for their detail, still exist. Besides his menial tasks, Marcus prepared negatives for proofing – a job for which the weekly wage was two shillings and sixpence. Having become familiar with the processes of photography he was allowed to sensitize the silver-albumenized paper for printing and varnishing the plates. Then he graduated to proofing and retouching, while continuing to polish the floors and brasses.

By this time Marcus Adams was enthusiastic about the whole process of photography and has described how he helped his sister Elsie in the various departments. He learnt to mount, cut and roll to obtain a good glaze with a hot press. (If too hot, it would melt the surface and spoil the print.) The prints were mostly cabinet and 'carte de visite' sizes. He experimented with tank-developing, and discovered a negative which could stand the test without streaking or fogging. Soon he had a tank built with vacuum sides to control the temperature, which held eighty exposures back to back. Developing them became a joy, rather than the previous loathsome task of hanging over flat dishes reeking of

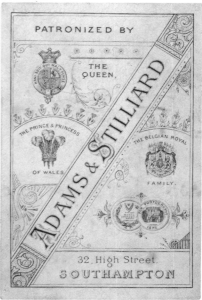

A typical business card (front and back) sent out by Walton Adams's studio in Southampton. Walton wrote in 1932, when he was over ninety: 'I believe that I am the oldest living British photographer. My first studio was opened in 1864. The greater part of my life since then has been spent in photography. I have in my time photographed about sixty thousand sitters and many strange tales and experiences have come my way. I had many noted people amongst my clientele, the most important being H. M. Queen Victoria. Another was General Gordon.'

pyro and ammonia. Later, during the First World War, he carried out tests for developing prints in tanks. Two six-foot sinks containing many gallons of water and diluted chemicals were used. He found a paper that stood twenty minutes' developing, with six or more exposures on a strip.

The years 1908 to 1913 were both constructive and inspired for Marcus Adams. In 1911 his first portraits were accepted by the London Salon of Photography. Two subjects, 'The Fairy Girl' and 'The Sunshine Boy', were published in *Photograms* in 1911. During this time he also developed a new style in children's pictures, which he called 'phase photography'. The child was taken in a number of positions which were arranged in sequence and printed on a single sheet of paper. Examples of these phase photographs may be seen at the beginning of chapters in this book.

It is noticeable that at about this time fewer adults were being exposed to the Marcus Adams camera. He had come to the conclusion that he had an increasing affinity and rapport with children; a gift which few photographers before him seem to have had. But as the war dragged on, business at the Reading studio, as far as child photography was concerned, slowly came to an end. Instead the Adams became involved in photographing men in the services. They opened a special studio near Reading station, 'The Khaki Studio', and another in the old Arcade. Thus there were three Adams studios within sight of Queen Victoria's statue near the Town Hall, along with many other photographers' studios. Marcus himself was involved only with 29 Blagrave Street.

When Adams was called up for war work (which in his case was drawing and painting aircraft in battle) he lodged in London at Featherstone Buildings, Holborn. Here he met and became a life-long friend of Ebenezer Howard, creator of the garden cities Letchworth and Welwyn. He was a frequent visitor to the Camera Club, where he met many photographers including Bertram Park, whose up-and-coming Society Photographic Studio in London he was soon to join. Whenever possible Marcus went home to Reading and, if the trains were not suitably timed, he would bicycle the forty miles each way.

The inventive years between 1890 and 1920 had been widely recognized and were important in providing a firm foundation and apprenticeship in general photography which would equip Marcus Adams for his specialized work in London.

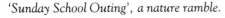
'Sunday School Outing', a nature ramble.

Marcus Adams felt he had reached a crucial stage in his professional career during the First World War. He wanted to break with his father and thought dimly about moving to London. But besides needing capital, he also sought his father's approval. Walton Adams was quick to reveal his anger. 'It is inconceivable that anyone should wish to work in a city full of wickedness,' he thundered, and threatened to sell the business and buy an annuity. A contract was nevertheless drawn up on 13 June 1919, breaking the partnership but allowing Marcus the interest from his children's pictures taken in Reading, and any fees due to him from his extensive collection of some six thousand negatives (glass plates) of Norman architecture made for Charles Keyser.

Meanwhile Bertram Park had left his London studio at the family home, 92 Fellowes Road, and with considerable difficulty obtained a lease on several rooms at 43 Dover Street, in Mayfair. No member of Park's family would lend him any money, but in 1915 he had managed to borrow £3,000 from the Earl of Carnarvon, who was a great friend and for whom he was later to do a series of nude photographs. Together with a colleague, Frank Buzzard, they formed a company to buy the Dover Street lease in 1916. Profits were quickly realized, and within a comparatively short time Park became distinguished for his portraits of society beauties. By this time he had met Marcus Adams several times at the Camera Club and had been down to the Reading studio and been impressed with his work. On 3 February 1919 Park wrote to Adams: '. . . if you ever make up your mind to come to London, I would be quite willing to consider a business arrangement with you, myself. Ever since I have got thoroughly on my legs here I have constantly refused to do portraits of children, and I am being continually asked to. It is a pity that the people I send away should drift along to Speaights and so on.'

This was the beginning of a forty-year partnership between Park and Adams. The initial development was to be mainly financed by Park, with Marcus Adams undertaking the children's sittings which Park considered himself less experienced and capable of carrying out.

The Nursery Studio began to take form in 1919. Adams was principally concerned with a sympathetic background for his child sitters. In striving to obtain an uninhibited likeness he thought it essential to avoid the nervous apprehension experienced by most children when going to the photographer. So his studio was designed to be as little as possible like a conventional one, with no visible cameras or tripods, no lamp standards or fearsome lights reminiscent of a dentist's surgery. From the moment they reached the studio on Dover Street, parents, nannies and children alike stepped into a new world.

Patterned manholes flanked the kerbside across the pavement. Some were coal-holes, others inspection covers used by the Electricity Board. Children, with their acute senses, noticed these. Once across the pavement, they entered a passage with a floor of blue-green mosaic and a showcase displaying a single child portrait. At the end of the passage was a mahogany door which led into a tiny lift in which four people, tightly packed, could ascend. Many children were not allowed in this but were taken up the stairs to the second floor and into a richly panelled, dimly

'Sunshine and Shadow', c. 1910. Probably taken on the Kennet and Avon canal, Reading.

Some of the trade marks and insignia designed by Marcus Adams and used on his mounts and writing paper.

lit reception room which served all three studios. A silk-overalled receptionist emerged from a room off the general office and conducted the visitors up more stairs to the floor above, where they were welcomed by Marcus Adams's studio assistants in a much lighter, more colourful reception area.

Adams maintained throughout his photographic career that colour played an important part in everyone's lives. 'Colour,' he wrote, 'can stimulate activity. The ancient peoples of Greece, India and the Far East understood the value of colour far more than we do. Red stimulates a quicker pulse and faster blood stream; green has great healing powers; gold and orange induce mental brightness; blue quietens the mind. Leonardo da Vinci declared that violet rays stimulated our powers of meditation. To violet we owe much in art and music and poetry; it works on the upper brain.' Although at that time it was not possible to produce colour photographs, Adams conceived a harmony of colour throughout his studio. The walls of the reception area were sunshine yellow, the high ceiling was of ultramarine blue. The furniture was natural-coloured sycamore on a grey carpet, and this scheme was continued into the outer area of the studio to which the family was next conducted. Here was a curtained-off and colourful dressing area where the mother, granny or nanny prepared the young for the sitting, which often involved a change of clothes. A wide glass screen divided this area from the studio, through which a riot of colour and toys, housed in tall glass cases, was visible.

The parents and nannies were asked to allow the children to wander into the studio and play with whatever toys they wished, thus becoming acclimatized to their surroundings before the arrival of Marcus Adams. A few parents were misguided enough to think this a waste of time, but most realized that it was an essential part of the child becoming relaxed.

Marcus Adams frequently arrived unobtrusively, clad in a pale, natural shantung overall. Any talk at this stage of the style of photograph or price was taboo. Adams considered that his duty was to make a portrait and he refused to take part in any business discussion. If the adults persisted, he was known to walk out and ask his secretary to cope with the details. There might, of course, be some discussion on change of dress at this stage.

Once inside the studio Adams would adjust his whole being to the age and mood of the child. This was no conscious effort but a natural identifiable mood. A platform might be moved, as if Adams were playing with large bricks, and more lights were switched on. (One boy demanded, 'Why can't you turn all those lights off and take your picture. Is there any need for so many?') The children helped, and meanwhile the studio assistant was busy behind a large Egyptian pedestal which concealed two cameras of revolutionary design. They were unrecognizable to most of the young, although one lad was heard to say, 'That's a camera to make pictures: you can't fool me.' Music played softly in the background while the playtime began, and the child was, unknowingly, enticed into the range of the mobile camera. A movable platform at one end of the studio was used to entertain the subject and,

A crowd gathering in Dover Street before a royal sitting. At centre left a determined Prince Charles can be seen marching towards the fun and games in Adams's studio.

Entrance to 43 Dover Street: The Three Studios. A limited number of prints was displayed in the window looking on to the street. There was little sign at the entrance of the excitement which a child would experience once he had arrived in the Marcus Adams Studio.

Typical press coverage for one of Marcus Adams's royal sittings, c. 1936. In this case the focus of attention was Prince Edward of Kent, aged two. This collection of pictures was pasted up in The Three Studios press agent's office of Miss Dorothy Clarke.

in some measure, concentrate movement into a small area. The whole space was lit by a series of light fittings placed at ceiling height down the screen divide and behind the camera. There was an overhead lantern with a 1500 watt lamp above the platform, which could be placed anywhere to focus on a figure or group. There was enough light, some 20,000 watts, to make a standard one-twelfth of a second exposure within the chosen decorative scheme.

The studio was not large, but intimate. A toy, stone or butterfly could be seen mounted in a case; a Victorian watch was ready to be held, and a walking stick was a popular prop. The conversation between photographer and child flowed, full of fun and humour. Throughout all this the subject was perhaps sitting high on a pedestal but completely oblivious of 'sitting still'. Adams insisted on focusing and constantly checking his ground-glass screen for composition, but all the time he was making his technical adjustments he kept up the play and conversation. Some parents, looking on through the screen, thought this procedure more of a spectacle than going to the theatre.

The point of all this fun and games was, however, to achieve a lasting record and a serene likeness of the child. The ideal that Marcus Adams sought was the radiant look of a child for its mother. This is wonderfully illustrated in his portrait of H.R.H. Princess Elizabeth (see p.120), brim full as it is with sparkle and affection.

The twenties heralded Marcus Adams's immediate success. Since the war parents had become less inclined to commission portraits of their children in watercolour, oils or pastel, and here, at last, was someone who could make a permanent record for the home under the scrutiny of the intuitive photographic eye. The classical portrait was, however, still much in Adams's mind, although he realized that photography had instant qualities that enabled a spontaneity denied to any but the greatest painters. During his years as a student, both at Reading University and in Paris, he had studied the beauty of paintings such as Fragonard's 'Fair Boy', and the Old Masters. Favourite artists he turned to again and again were Reynolds, Rowney, Gainsborough, Raeburn, Titian, Franz Hals and Luini. Frequently he looked to them for inspiration, and they came under his critical, perceptive eye. It was from these painters' portrayal of children that he drew most satisfaction, and in some instances he tried to emulate them by capturing their style in a photograph (see, for example, p.66). A Rembrandt-like quality of light, nobility and simplicity and a certain timeless feeling became the hallmark of an Adams picture. Cecil Beaton, writing in *The Magic Image*, summed it up thus: 'By simple means, Marcus Adams made romantic, Raeburnesque portraits of little girls on a heather moor, with storm cloud backgrounds.' There is no doubt that his portraits of the twenties and thirties in this style had this very painterly quality of luminosity and directness.

In 1925 the American magazine *The Camera* gave this account of the artist behind the lens.

No painter, including Titian and Holbein, Rembrandt and Reynolds, as well as those of our own time, has given the world child studies in such beautiful variety as Marcus Adams, and if anything is calculated to inspire lovers of the camera to insist on the national recognition of its great artists, it is pictures such as those which we have the privilege of presenting to our readers.

A fact beyond dispute, yet nevertheless one little realised even by contemporary photographers, is that these child pictures of Marcus Adams' creation are, without exception, not 'likenesses' but character studies of rare beauty and consummate skill. Anybody can produce a likeness, and the radiant beauty of childhood is for all to behold and to delight in. But to discover and portray the soul demands genius. . . .

Mr Adams is a toiler, and he is completely saturated with love for his work, and when I describe him as a genius I mean simply that his work is the product of these two factors.

Marcus Adams did not always have complete freedom with his subjects. There were times when parents' instructions had to be observed, and so he would first make his picture meet that requirement, then, if opportunity allowed, he would please himself – and frequently more than please his patron.

When making pictures of older children, many interesting and sometimes highly technical discussions would take place, resulting in the young enthusiast being shown the workroom and the various processes. The essential part of the studio contact was to create an atmosphere in which the child could give of its best in a normal, disciplined manner. There were moments when, having stimulated the child to a point of joyful hilarity, it became necessary for Adams to calm him down again, especially when toys and objects were being flung in all directions. (In the summer, when the windows were open, toys were often to be seen hurtling through space down three floors to the street below.) However, patience and psychological control seemed a natural element in Marcus Adams's structure. The noisy boisterousness would be transformed to whispers and an exchange of confidences, and thus the portrait was captured.

Marcus Adams described what happened when the child entered the studio.

There is perfect liberty and any toy may be chosen. It is not many seconds before a dead set is made for the favourite, and one young lady said: 'Oh, Mummy, can I buy all these toys and take them home?' to which her mother replied, 'You may play with them but they belong to an Uncle.' 'Shall I see him?' 'Yes, he will be here in a few minutes.' By the time I arrive they are fully engaged in arranging everything and putting the dollies to bed, or some other game of pretence. On my arrival it is my turn to enter into the fun they have started and lead their interest to the spot I desire to make the picture. The fun begins and probably goes on until I have accomplished my task, maybe an hour or less; I then gradually ease off and get them to help me to tidy up. The lights slowly go out and

all is quiet. It is often said that surely this is the brightest, happiest room in London.

The difference between the ordinary run-of-the-mill photographers' results and the Marcus Adams photograph is well summed up by his son:

> He created a scene and situation into which he placed his subject, then, with his unique understanding of children, he stimulated expressions to obtain his ultimate ideal. The design of the Adams picture was important in relation to the surrounding of the subject. He used considerable quantities of negative stock which were quite beyond those costs of the commercially run studio. Perhaps this was the big difference between the Marcus Adams portraits and those of other studios, which used every known means to stimulate business. His photographs were always in demand.

There was no doubt that Marcus Adams possessed mystical qualities which extended beyond his interest in phrenology, palmistry and psychology. It was later discovered that he had an uncanny understanding of the supernatural. His technical ability was so ingrained that ninety-five per cent of the time he spent with the subject was devoted to psychology. It was here that Marcus Adams showed his real genius.

It should be appreciated that at the time Marcus Adams was enjoying his somewhat rapid success in the twenties as a result of his move to London, he was already fifty years old, an age when less active men would be preparing for retirement. To Adams this was just the beginning. He always maintained that he owed a great deal to the constant encouragement of his sitters, not least the enthusiasm and patronage of the Royal Family. He enjoyed meeting people whose knowledge could add to his own, and he wrote: 'I love digging into a fresh mind and discovering from it the trend of growth and what it cultivates mentally. It's astonishing what you find buried beneath the mere features of a face.'

His home environment was also a stabilizing influence on his life. Although he changed houses on a number of occasions he always lived in the Reading area, from where he travelled some 24,000 miles annually to his work. Gardening was a constant pleasure: he planned and landscaped gardens and planted trees wherever he lived, and won prizes for his sweet peas. He always had a studio workshop in which he would manufacture his own woodwork tools, polishing them until they had a perfect surface. He carved and sculpted stone, painted in oil, watercolour and pastel, and did many hundreds of drawings.

Marcus Adams's love of the countryside and wildflowers led him to produce a wealth of drawings of trees and watercolours of landscapes. His preoccupation with the Sunday School in his younger days encouraged him to walk some miles to church twice or three times on a Sunday; although, when he purchased a car, the countryside took precedence over active religion.

Adams travelled extensively, mostly with his wife, Lily Maud, sometimes alone, and often with his brother Chris. The latter companion was a great joy to him. The Middle East, Africa, southern Europe, Paris, Switzerland and Italy were his most frequent destinations. On his first trip by boat to Syria in 1901 he encouraged all those he met with a camera to have their negatives processed in the Reading studio, thus quadrupling business within a short space of time. Foreign travel was a highlight of his life and provided him with experience to impart to his little sitters. He owed his energetic output to his own creative environment, to his friends and to the loyalty of his patrons.

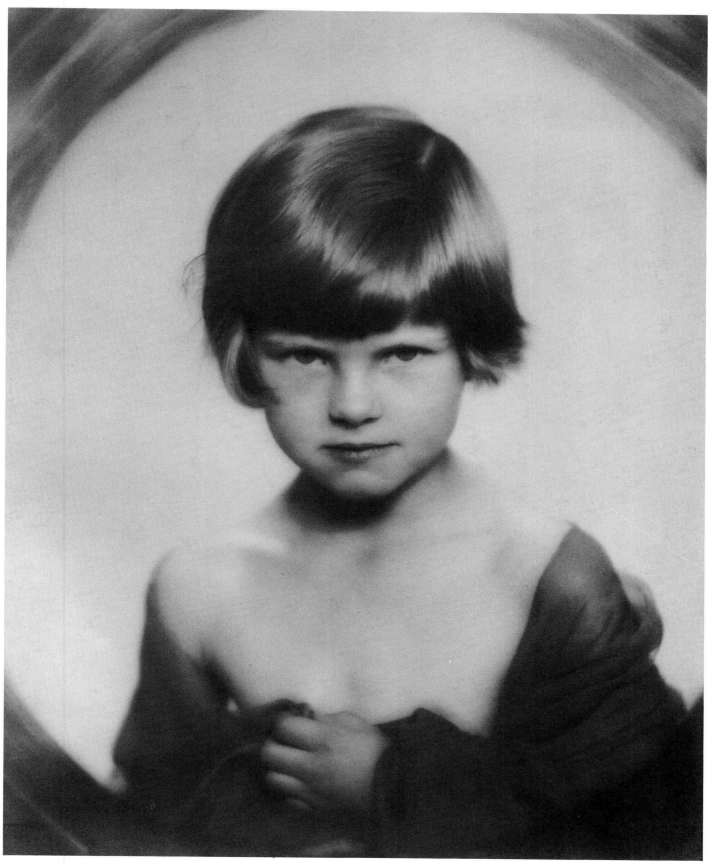

WONDERMENT
Portrait of one of the Eller sisters
13⅘ × 11⅒in (34 × 28.2 cm)

PORTRAIT OF A YOUNG GIRL, *c.* 1910
11⁹⁄₁₀ × 8⁴⁄₅in (30.2 × 22.3 cm)

'We all know wherein lies the art of photographing a child – it is,
to make a natural picture.' *Pearsons Magazine*, 1911

WINDING UP MY AEROPLANE, *c.* 1910
12 × 9⅗in (30.5 × 24.3cm)

'The little one was not harassed in any way by the camera, which was hidden in a corner forming a stall for toys. In fact everything appeared to be provided – from a huge rocking-horse to a teddy bear, and from lively little goldfish to wonderful flying machines – in order to attract the attention and afford pleasure to the children.' *Reading Mercury,* 1913

PORTRAIT STUDY OF A BOY
11½ × 8⁷⁄₁₀in (29.2 × 22cm)

PORTRAIT OF THE BRACKLEY CHILDREN, MARY, JOHN
AND DAVID, 1929
7⁹⁄₁₀ × 6in (20 × 15.2cm)

A characteristic of Marcus Adams was his ability to arrange a
group and capture it in a fraction of a second. The build-up to
such a picture, however, might take an hour or more.

PORTRAIT OF A YOUNG GIRL
13½ × 10in (34.3 × 25.4cm)

THE GOLDFISH BOWL, *c.* 1912
11³⁄₅ × 8⁴⁄₅in (29.5 × 22.4cm)

PORTRAIT OF A GIRL CAPTIVATED BY THE
PHOTOGRAPHER'S PLAYTIME
9²⁄₅ × 11¹⁄₅in (23.9 × 28.4 cm)

Taken about the same time as 'The Goldfish Bowl', the
photograph is full of vitality and alertness and already shows the
mastery Adams achieved in catching an expression.

PORTRAIT OF A GIRL
5⁹/₁₀ × 7⁹/₁₀in (15 × 20cm)

PORTRAIT OF A CHILD
Late 19th century
7⁴/₅ × 5⁷/₁₀in (19.8 × 14.5cm)

'Not by any haphazard snap-shooting could these and such pictures be made. To the making of them went love and understanding of children, the soul of an artist.' *Pearsons Magazine*, 1911

SUSPICION AND ANGER
10⁷/₁₀ × 8⁷/₁₀in (27.2 × 22cm)

Sometimes children's tempers would outwit even Marcus Adams's psychology. In the summer the smart Dover Street passers-by would suddenly find themselves showered with fluffy rabbits, parrots and goldfish flung out of the windows. After many such incidents heavy glass panels were hung outside, preventing the toys leaving the studio but allowing the windows to be kept open.

THE BISHOP
13 × 9½in (33 × 24.1cm)

PORTRAIT OF A CHILD
14⅕ × 11in (36 × 27.9cm)

'I remember one child of three and a half who stood solidly in the
middle of my studio and would not yield to any inducements to
play or talk – a hopeless position. I left the studio, told the nurse
to have a good romp and that I would return in ten to fifteen
minutes. When I returned matters were different. All was well.
Afterwards I discovered mother had told the child to stand still for
a photograph and do as the man told her. When the child was free
and happy the whole atmosphere was perfect and we had a lovely
time.' Marcus Adams broadcast, 1939

PORTRAIT OF A CHILD
13½ × 10½in (34.3 × 26.7cm)

PORTRAIT OF A CHILD
13⁹⁄₁₀ × 10⁷⁄₁₀in (35.3 × 27.1cm)

With the slow photographic material and with little or no depth
of focus it was essential to keep the subject in one position for a
limited amount of time, but as well as keeping the body static
Adams required the expression to be alive and alert.

PORTRAIT OF A BOY IN SMOCK
13½ × 10⅕in (34.3 × 25.9cm)

PORTRAIT OF A CHILD
11⅕ × 8⁷⁄₁₀in (28.4 × 22cm)

A PROVOCATIVE POSE
10²⁄₅ × 8²⁄₅in (26.4 × 21.3cm)

'Everybody knows that there is a time in the history of every artist
when he is at his best, and that inspiration is oftentimes a matter
even of moments.' *The Camera*, 1925

SHY GLANCE, 1920
June Park, daughter of Adams's partner, Bertram Park
13³⁄₁₀ × 10¹⁄₅in (33.8 × 25.9cm)
Collection Mrs Mardall

Adams was asked to photograph June every year until she was
twenty-one.

CHRISTOPHER MILNE, MARCH 1928
Son of the author A. A. Milne and subject of his well-loved
children's books
8 × 6in (20.3 × 15.2cm)
Collection National Portrait Gallery

Christopher Robin remembers Marcus Adams 'looking a little like
Einstein and speaking in a delicate, high and gentle voice,
perhaps a little foreign. Wherein lay his success? I don't know. He
may have been technically brilliant. He may have had the right
society connections. As far as I was concerned, he was gentle and
kind and any expertise was well hidden behind the manner of a
pleasantly bumbling, rather foolish old man.'

MISCHIEF BREWING IN COVENT GARDEN
14⅘ × 11⅕in (37.6 × 30cm)

The costumes were designed for a Vacani Matinée.

PORTRAIT STUDY OF A CHILD IN THE OLD MASTER
TRADITION
7½ × 5⁷⁄₁₀in (19 × 14.5cm)

'To photograph with any degree of success we must have studied the Old Masters of all the arts. Painters in oils provide a vast field for seeking knowledge as to the details of picture-making, whilst the etcher should not be neglected because of the definite line by which he must express his intentions. But in advising anyone to get inspiration I would add that it is undesirable merely to copy and imitate. We must find our own way and be our distinctive selves and let our own personality dominate all our work.'
Marcus Adams in *The Amateur Photographer*, 1924

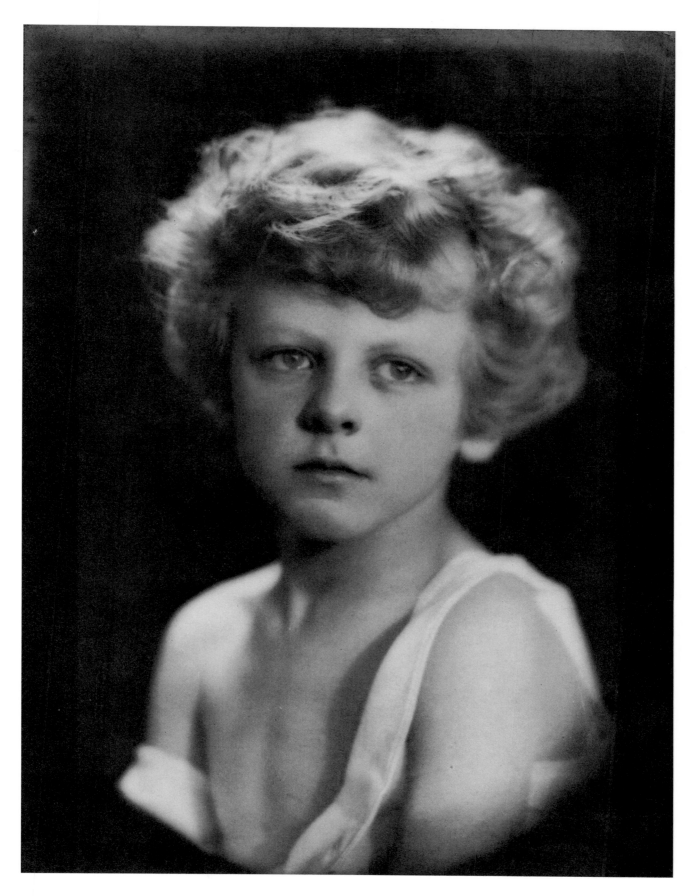

PORTRAIT OF A BOY
14²/₅ × 10¹/₅in (36.6 × 25.9cm)

THE SONG
12½ × 11in (31.7 × 27.9cm)

CHAPTER

II

EQUIPMENT AND TECHNIQUES

'The essential of a perfect picture is *simplicity*. The delightful simplicity of a child calls for a simple pictorial statement. Oh, the difficulty of portraying that wonder of a child's expression! The face is but the outward shape and form.'

The Three Studios at 43 Dover Street, used by Marcus Adams, Bertram Park and his wife Yvonne Gregory, had one communal works, though each had its own individual technicians who used the same processing facilities. Marcus Adams not only took the picture of the child, but himself supervised every stage of the production until the finished print was finally signed and despatched.

Over fifty processes were involved from the moment of booking an appointment to the finished portrait, many of them highly skilled and requiring specialized training. The quality that Marcus Adams demanded was attained through a mixture of precision, sensitivity and intuition.

A careful balance of tonal and focal quality was achieved by using a combination of lenses in the camera. The negative stock was Barnet orthochromatic matte-emulsion H&D 700, manufactured by Elliott & Sons Ltd. The plate was developed in home-mixed Metol Hydrokinone solution, adjusted in formula for each batch of plates delivered, and tank-developed in racks containing eighty plates, packed back to back.

The plates were allowed to dry naturally and were then examined and selected by Marcus Adams, who seldom trusted anyone else with that job. The proportion to be printed was scribed on the matte negative, again by himself. The plates were numbered and proofed and there was little or no retouching as we know it.

The proofs were made in specially built teak horizontal enlargers, using a 10½ inch Cooke lens with adjustable soft focus. The light source in the large boxes was mercury M tube, from Hewettic. Printing was on Kodura E paper Chlorobromide, initially coated to Marcus Adams's personal specification and later marketed to the profession. Each batch of paper varied considerably, so whole coatings were purchased and cut to Adams's requirements. Later, the paper deteriorated in quality, partly due to too much Byrata (china clay filling) preventing the emulsion from penetrating the paper. However, there was no better stock available and when, after the Second World War, Kodak ceased making the paper, Adams in his ceaseless quest for perfection thought that he should give up photography.

Throughout the whole period of the Dover Street partnership, Marcus Adams remained remarkably consistent in his requirements. Once the ordered prints had been checked against the proofs for position and alterations, they were placed in a named folio for scrutiny and approval by Adams, who liked to have the printer by his side at this time

Amaryllis Fleming, now a distinguished cellist, dressed as an oyster for a Vacani Matinée.

All the negative stock was on glass and coated with a matte emulsion. This made it possible to draw on the surface with black plumbago powder using a chamois leather stump. The drawing of black will ultimately print light. Much of the design of this photograph, and many of those taken for Madame Vacani's annual theatre shows, and others for charity matinées, was built up in this manner for the press.

to answer any questions. If all was well with the previous day's output then the folio with its prints and proofs was moved to another floor where spotting and finish were completed, before going to yet another floor to be hot-dry mounted under heavy presses on to a specially adapted mount card. Until 1940 these mounts were made from material manufactured with its own watermark and folded by Messrs Jeffcoat. The paper was generally ordered by the ton. To preserve the surface of the print the mounted photograph was protected by a thin tissue folder and sealed with a red seal.

Before this seal was fixed the photograph was signed personally by Marcus Adams, signifying his approval. There were times however when the order, or part of it, was rejected by him, which might mean the whole process being done all over again. This high standard was appreciated by the team, who responded sympathetically to Marcus Adams; some said how exciting it was to work for such a man. He never stinted his praise for work well done, and saw it as a crime not to work for this highest achievement.

The staff at the Walton Adams Studio in Reading. (Collection National Portrait Gallery)

However much store Adams set by his equipment, he nevertheless believed that it should be subordinate to the sitting. Everything had to be manipulated in the simplest, most automatic manner to allow him to concentrate wholeheartedly on his sitter, although automation of camera equipment in the twenties and thirties as described by Adams could hardly be compared to the computerized cameras of the eighties. He had already devised a camera for the Reading studio which was built into a cavity in the wall, into which his technician, or assistant, could walk to change the plates and keep it in focus. The London camera he conceived was slightly different, although it too was an obscure piece of equipment which very few people (particularly children) recognized as a camera.

Adams required a camera which was easy to work while fulfilling the purpose for which it was designed. He stated that most of the cameras built were quite useless for children's photography, being very clumsy in their operation. 'The shutters are enough to scare the life out of a child; besides, I contend that a camera should be so constructed that it's a part of the person using it.' He went on to say that all those that he designed and made 'did not have the customary old-fashioned black cloth where you hide your face and disarrange your hair!' 'Another

The Marcus Adams Studio at 43 Dover Street, London. The Edwardian finery of the front of house staff in Reading (opposite) contrasts dramatically with the practical shantung silk overalls worn by all workroom and reception personnel at Dover Street. Many of the Dover Street staff had interchangeable duties, although some were very skilled and worked for all three separate studios of Marcus Adams, Bertram Park and Yvonne Gregory.

disadvantage of the ordinary instrument,' wrote Adams, 'is mounting it on a three-legged tripod.' Instead it should be made to rise and fall, in the same way as a sash-cord window, from 2 feet to 6 feet, functioning noiselessly and with little physical effort. Screws and knobs which enabled one to adjust the swing and tilt of the lens or back of the camera were ineffectual when working with the speed of a child's mobility – added to which, these adjustments led to some measure of distortion. Consequently, Adams kept the back of the camera with the plate rigid while adjusting the lens, which was mounted in a ball and socket engineered casting, similar to that of the human eyeball, which could be swivelled universally.

After years of experimenting, Adams succeeded in contriving perfect movements with his apparatus. The principle of the camera caused much controversy with his colleagues. He was so confident of his scientific development in moving the lens as in an eyeball that he often wondered why the trade did not make a similar camera. No doubt the reason was the cost. Some of the subjects he wanted to take would have been impossible without the front adjustment. Two of the strangest cameras he ever designed involved the person who operated them standing inside to work the focus and the plates, entirely in the dark.

The London camera was a twin-lens type which enabled Adams to focus through one lens while the other worked in concert. Unfortunately he could not find in London a matched pair of lenses that gave true focus at all points. Instead, one side was used for full-length portraits and the other for head shots and three-quarter figures, but using a patent movable front lens in the ball and socket with an Eastman plate adaptor on the back. The lenses were used long-focus for close-up work: 15 inch Dallmeyer 4.5 to cover half-plate size negatives and 10 inch Tessar for full length. The operator moved about with twenty feet of rubber tubing which operated a butterfly-wing Dallmeyer shutter, giving about one-twelfth of a second when squeezed. The constant need to focus required the shutter to be opened and yet be in instant operation without cocking. The half-plate Kodak back took double-sided plate holders which could be changed rapidly by a studio assistant. Two hundred exposures an hour could be made if speed were necessary. During a busy session it was not unusual for a thousand glass negatives to be processed in a day.

Cartoonists' views of Marcus Adams. In the picture (right) Spurrier shows the so-called hidden camera with the two lenses under a shelf on which were placed plants and toys. A slightly later cartoon by Ern Shaw (opposite) has Adams down on the floor with his subject.

An interesting camera designed by Marcus Adams was one which enabled him to travel with his apparatus. The camera was packed in a box for wartime visits to family homes. In addition, there were two chromium-plated rods for carrying the cradle on which the actual part was fixed. The rods were screwed into the container box to ensure that they were upright and parallel. The camera was built with many bits and pieces from his personal workshop so that it slid perfectly up and down. Again the ball and socket principle was used. A leather-covered card with a central hole in which to fix a magnifying glass acted as a cover for the screen, instead of the usual black focusing cloth. The double box body container had spring-loaded runners for focusing to allow smooth action when operated by a quadrant and handle. All cameras he designed were focused by means of a handle working on a quadrant. The 15 × 15 inch container did not permit a base for castors, so Adams worked out a simple method of extending them a further 4-5 inches, thus avoiding any wobble. In spite of being rather heavy, the camera was easy to carry with two loop handles. The only items that Adams bought

The travelling camera invented by Marcus Adams.

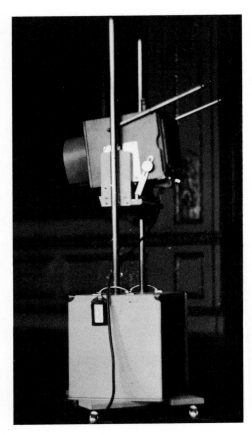

The travelling camera set to expose.

to make this camera were the four castors, two handles and some brass screws. Vital parts, such as the adaptor for plates, lens and shutter, he already had. The body of the camera was of similar construction to the first ever made by Fox Talbot of Lacock.

One of Marcus Adams's bitterest moments was when he returned to his studio after a long bout of ill-health during the 1940s, only to find that his partner had replaced his camera with one Adams considered totally unworkable. It is arguable, however, whether this made any real difference to the quality of his photographs, as the final prints lost little of the excellence which he had strived for in the twenties and thirties. However, thereafter the pictures were taken with a great deal more effort and consciousness. It is probable that Bertram Park in 1945 thought Marcus Adams was ready to retire, as he was over seventy, but instead of doing this he continued for a further twelve years. Marcus Adams also discovered, at that time, that thousands of his glass negatives had been removed from the filing store and sent to the dump. This unfortunate action had destroyed some of this finest work which was intended for exhibition. He never felt the same about his business partner again, and explored many ways of dissolving the partnership.

Yet in spite of its ups and downs, its periods of agreement and disagreement, the partnership held together through a web of true talent combined with business acumen. That it endured for so many years is remarkable when one considers the strength of the personalities of the major participants.

JACQUELINE DE BROGLIO
Daughter of the Hon. Mrs Reginald (Daisy) Fellowes
14½ × 10½in (36.8 × 26.7cm)

THE WOOD NYMPH, 1925
Aline, daughter of Mrs Duncanson
14 × 10³⁄₁₀in (35.6 × 26.2cm)

In this picture Marcus Adams has invented an imaginary woodland setting with natural grasses and silver birch, flowers, stones and twigs. He never failed to find an opportunity to use his painterly talents. He would often rough out on a sheet of paper an arrangement of how he would like to see the final picture. He would then stage-design the picture in the studio, carefully placing his subject in the appropriate position.

THE DRAGONFLY, 1938
Virginia, daughter of Mrs Vernon Tate
13⅕ × 11in (33.5 × 27.9cm)

GRANIA GUINNESS AGED NINE, 1929
8 × 6in (20.3 × 15.2cm)

Grania is wearing her bridesmaid's dress for the marriage of her
cousin Oonagh Guinness to the Hon. Philip Kindersley. She was
one of Marcus Adams's very special sitters.

LADY MARY STEWART
14 × 10in (35.6 × 25.4cm)

STUDY OF TWO YOUNG LADIES PREPARED FOR
EQUESTRIAN SPORT
14 × 10in (35.6 × 25.4cm)

JEREMY WILSON, 1929
Son of Mrs Guy Wilson
9³⁄₁₀ × 6⁷⁄₁₀in (23.6 × 17cm)

RICHARD BEAUMONT, 1930
Son of Lady Allendale
7⁹⁄₁₀ × 6in (20 × 15.2cm)

DICK PAGET COOKE, 1926
7⁹⁄₁₀ × 6in (20 × 15.2cm)

DAVID WATTS RUSSELL, 1924
8 × 6in (20.3 × 15.2cm)

PORTRAIT OF A BOY
14²⁄₅ × 9⁹⁄₁₀in (36.6 × 25.1cm)

'Art is an ideal made evident in form and shape, whether it be applied to a painting, etching, or any other mode of graphic expression. Photography being the youngest of these modes, new methods must be discovered to bring into close application the rules and feelings of art.' Marcus Adams in *The Amateur Photographer*, 1924

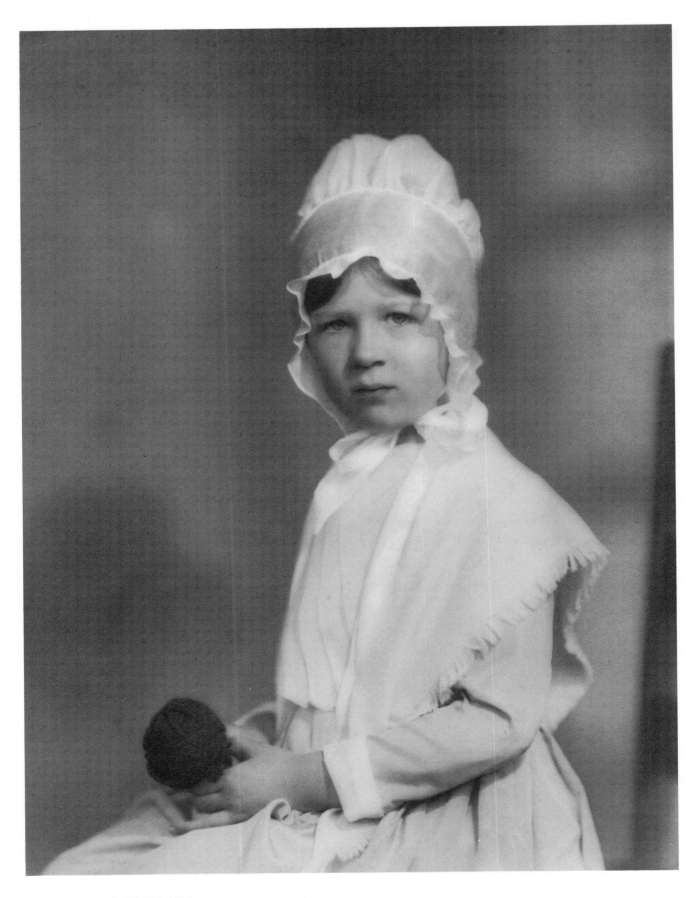

ELFRIDA HUNTINGDON, 1928
13⁷⁄₁₀ × 10³⁄₁₀in (34.8 × 26.2cm)

RICHARD CHAPLIN, 1920
Son of Mrs Vere Chaplin
14 × 11in (35.6 × 27.9cm)

Considering the difficulties of slow exposure times it is quite remarkable that Adams was able to capture the entranced look on the baby's face. Marcus Adams's son Gilbert was later to photograph Richard Chaplin's baby in similar costume.

LADY MARY PONSONBY, 1927
The Countess of Bessborough's daughter
14¹⁄₁₀ × 10¹⁄₁₀in (35.8 × 25.7cm)

HAZEL BELVILLE, 1929
7⁹⁄₁₀ × 6in (20 × 15.2cm)

PATRICIA CALVERT DRESSED AS A VICTORIAN LADY,
1929
7⁹⁄₁₀ × 6in (20 × 15.2cm)

VIRGINIA HUTCHINSON AS MARIE ANTOINETTE, 1935
14¾ × 10⁹⁄₁₀in (37.5 × 27.7cm)

Bernard Shaw, when viewing this picture, thought it the finest
portrait he had ever seen.

MARTYN AND MARIGOLD BEVAN, 1938
13 × 10in (33 × 25.4cm)

Aug. 2, 1922   *Sketch*   169

The Lord Chancellor's Younger Daughter as a Reynolds.

"POSED AS "LADY GERTRUDE FITZPATRICK," BY SIR JOSHUA REYNOLDS: THE HON. PAMELA SMITH.

The beautiful child on this page is shown posed as Sir Joshua Reynolds's famous portrait of Lady Gertrude Fitzpatrick, and the result is a splendid example of modern photographic art. The Hon. Pamela Smith, who is the subject of the picture, is the younger daughter of the Lord High Chancellor, Viscount Birkenhead, and of Viscountess Birkenhead. She was born in 1914, and is the youngest member of the family. Her brother, the Hon. Frederick Smith, is seven years her senior; and her sister, the Hon. Eleanor Smith, is one of the most popular girls in Society.

PORTRAIT STUDY EXCLUSIVE TO "THE SKETCH";
By *Marcus Adams, The Children's Studio, 43, Dover Street, W.*

THE HON. PAMELA SMITH, 1922
$10\frac{4}{5} \times 8\frac{2}{5}$in (26.4 × 21.3cm)

A similar picture of the younger daughter of Viscount Birkenhead, the Lord High Chancellor, was published in *Sketch*.

PORTRAIT OF A GIRL SET IN A GAINSBOROUGH-LIKE
BACKGROUND
14³⁄₁₀ × 11²⁄₅in (36.3 × 28.9cm)

DAVID WATTS RUSSELL, 1919
7⁹⁄₁₀ × 6in (20 × 15.2cm)

F. C. Tilney wrote in *Photograms of the Year*, 1920: 'What a
portrait for a doting mother to cherish! Marcus Adams has been to
the fore this year in his children's portraits, of which David is a
good sample of his artistic treatment.'

PORTRAIT OF A GIRL
11 × 10½in (27.9 × 26.7cm)

'This is not flattery. It is obvious truth. And if you would verify it, take these very pictures to any mother, rich or poor, common or cultured, and you need never ask her to express an opinion. The mother's heart within her will respond to their appeal as the flower to the sun.' *The Camera*, 1925

PORTRAIT OF A GIRL, *c.* 1910
13³⁄₁₀ × 10¹⁄₁₀in (33.8 × 25.6cm)

Probably taken in the Reading studio, using no visible props save in this instance the heavy velvet curtains.
'How seldom do photographs show the natural joy of childhood! Most children are thoroughly frightened by the time their photographer working on approved lines – possibly an awe-inspiring stranger with a vast and terrifying apparatus beside him – has finished posing them. The aim of a happy child's picture should be a happy effect – this natural happiness, with no stiff convention, is far more becoming and true to childish nature than any other studied effect. To understand a child is the beginning of wisdom in child photography.' *Pearsons Magazine*, 1911

CAROLYNE THYNNE, 1931
Daughter of the Marquess of Bath, now the Duchess of Beaufort
14¹⁄₁₀ × 9⁷⁄₁₀in (35.8 × 24.6cm)

Adams has carefully arranged the balance of composition in this portrait. A similar portrait hangs in the Long Drawing Room at Longleat House.
(Reproduced by kind permission of the Marquess of Bath)

PORTRAIT OF A CHILD AT HOME
14³⁄₁₀ × 11in (36.3 × 27.9cm)

The picture was taken during the Second World War when it was
thought too dangerous for children to travel to London and
Marcus Adams visited homes all over Britain with his portable
camera.

PORTRAIT OF A CHILD
14 × 11in (35.6 × 27.9cm)

ANN CHEVALIER PARKER
7⁹⁄₁₀ × 6in (20 × 15.2cm)

STUDIO PORTRAIT OF A BOY WITH BUTTON SHOES
AND PANDORA'S BOX
11⅕ × 8⅓in (28.4 × 20.8cm)

This photograph was taken between 1900 and 1910 when Marcus
Adams was beginning to establish his reputation for child
photography in Reading. Adams has focused the boy's attention
on the simple collection of toys placed on the small table. Note
the wagon about to fall off the pedestal.

PORTRAIT OF A GIRL WITH A PARROT
14⅕ × 11in (36 × 27.9cm)

PORTRAIT OF A BOY WITH A PEKINESE
14⅕ × 11⅕in (36 × 28.4cm)

A comment by the studio assistant on the reverse of the
photograph reads: 'Pets were often brought to the studio.'

BOY WITH ROCKING HORSE, *c.* 1908
12 × 9⅘in (30.5 × 24.8cm)

Considering the speed and action of the subject, Marcus Adams
conveys his skill in obtaining an almost in-focus print when
taking into account the slow-speed materials available at the
time.

CHAPTER
III
THE END OF AN IDEAL

'I am fond of children, fond of art, and love creating pictures. I realized in early years that the medium of photography was the best method of recording the fleeting expressions that glow over a child's face.'

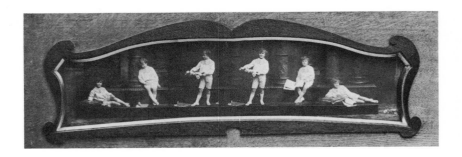

After the Second World War, Marcus Adams had declared: 'If Kodak cease making my special paper, I shall stop taking photographs.' This proved to be a serious threat, and though he continued to work for another few years he did try to give up when the paper was withdrawn. Several people with technical expertise from leading photographic firms helped Adams in his quest for suitable materials, among whom was Tony Greenwood of Elliotts of Barnet. Batches of test paper would arrive at Dover Street, but in many cases it was found unsuitable for Adams's exacting requirements. During the post-war period, Dr Mullins and Leslie Beck of Kodak were finding it hard to persuade Adams to accept what was then available. Adams would not tolerate an inferior paper. Both these experts look back on the Kodak meetings with distant amusement. In spite of his demands, Adams was greatly respected.

In the fifties, a fellow-photographer predicted that as soon as grand pianos were withdrawn from the average drawing-room people would no longer wish to be photographed by studio photographers. There was some truth in this. More significant, however, was the arrival of the automatic camera which most fathers, and some mothers, were beginning to possess, making the snapshot increasingly available and popular. The more haphazard home photography, although it lacked classical and lasting qualities, was considered quite sufficient as a record of the growing family in a somewhat austere post-war economic period. Apart from 1951, a year in which Marcus Adams seems to have had one of his periodic breakdowns, the largest part of the business at the Dover Street Three Studios derived from the work of Marcus Adams and his assistant James Vintner. Bertram Park's contribution to Three Studios became negligible after the war. He took less and less interest in active studio life, and yet he expected his partner not only to carry on the sittings with Vintner but also to keep a close eye on the distribution of the profits.

Perhaps the saddest period of Marcus Adams's successful career with children was towards the middle of the fifties. It became increasingly apparent that Adams and Park, who had both enjoyed their individual glory, were now being forced to recognize their differences. Their partnership resembled that of Gilbert and Sullivan: they worked together but never understood one another. Park assumed an increasingly dictatorial approach, and even his daughter readily admits that he did become very high-handed towards the end of his career when

Composite studies such as this one of Lady Churston and her daughters (see also p. 83), published in Sketch, *were popular in the twenties and thirties.*

he claimed that it was his money that kept the business going. He would often say he was quite willing to give Marcus Adams his help, provided the latter did not interfere with the business side. The truth is that although Adams was a photographer of considerable inspiration and talent – as Park himself was – in the early stages of the partnership it was Park who provided the business acumen that allowed them to survive. Later on however, when Park found other interests, it was Adams who kept the business alive.

At the age of seventy Marcus Adams was still determined to continue his photographic career, but many factors combined to change the circumstances in which he worked. The greatest of these were social ones: the war had made a mark from which many families would never recover. The London 'season' almost ceased. Photography now centred on the quick snapshot. The Dover Street premises became more and more expensive, while the other two studios did little to pay their way. Marcus Adams was becoming increasingly disenchanted with working to maintain the property and facilities. Ultimately he continued to play with children and take photographs just for the fun of it.

Throughout Marcus Adams's career, photography by his contemporaries was being judged and criticized on its pictorial merit. It was seen principally by the critics as an art form, at times as a substitute for painting. This, after all, is what those pioneers in photography had in some measure sought to accomplish. Critics said of the Marcus Adams picture that 'an Adams never grows old because the touch of the Master shows through', and, 'he has created a style of his own which has kept up with the times without losing its character.'

Marcus Adams by Gilbert Adams, 1955. The photograph was taken on the terrace of the Adams home, Lavender Cottage, overlooking the Thames, to commemorate Marcus Adams's eightieth birthday.

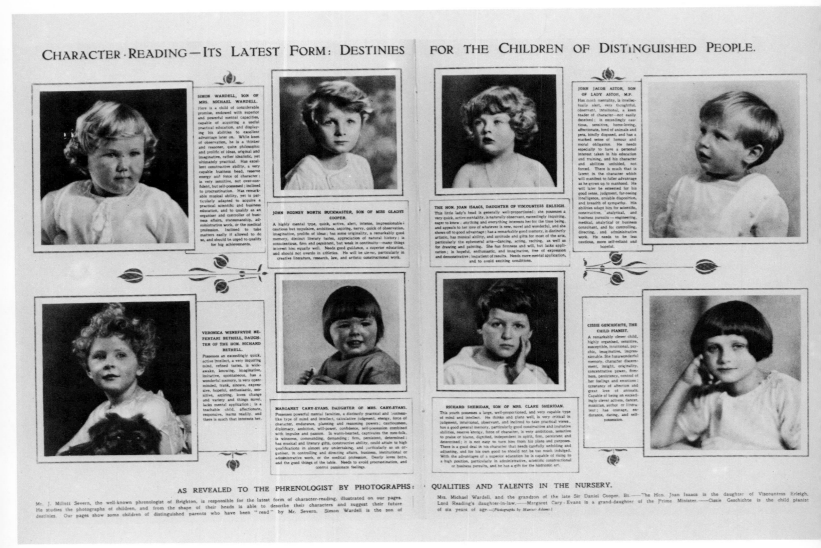

Pages from Sketch, *4 May 1921 (above) and 11 February 1925.*

Marcus Adams, for most of his years, actively worked towards improving the status and conditions of his fellow-photographers. He greatly valued the friendship of F. J. Mortimer and, later, George Halford, and he had a particular interest in his assistants and staff engaged in photography. Much co-operation took place within the Photographers' Professional Association. Adams was engaged on the promotion of the members' regular publication and spent much time on designing and setting it. He attended hundreds of committee and council meetings, and became President of the association in 1925. During his term of office he toured Britain, speaking on photography and encouraging improvements in standards. He also became a member and later a Fellow of the Royal Photographic Society, an institution which covered the whole spectrum of photographic sciences. His particular contribution was in the pictorial section. His friendship with Herbert Lambert of Bath and F. J. Mortimer soon involved him in the newly formed London Salon. His work appeared regularly in their Pall Mall Exhibition and, eventually, at the Royal Watercolour Society, which became the Salon's home. It was Adams's tireless endeavours,

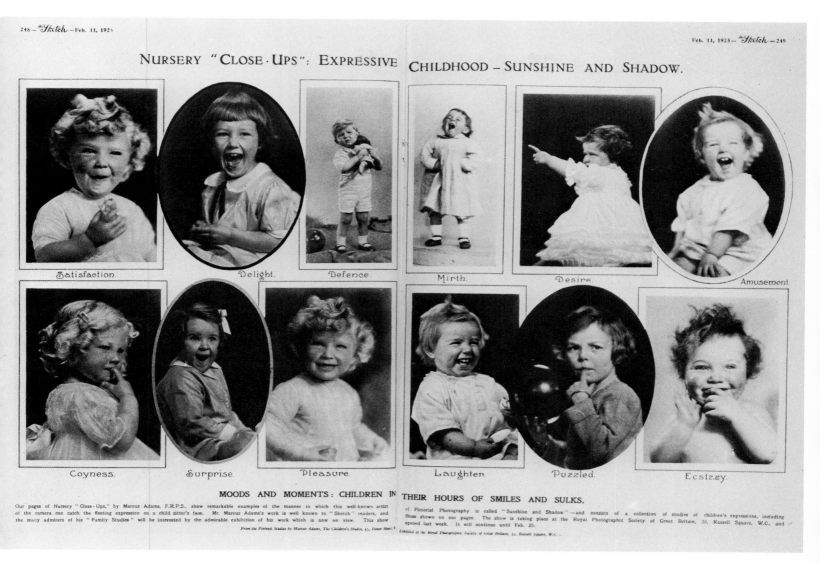

248 – "Sketch" – Feb. 11, 1925

Feb. 11, 1925 – "Sketch" – 249

NURSERY "CLOSE-UPS": EXPRESSIVE CHILDHOOD – SUNSHINE AND SHADOW.

Satisfaction. Delight. Defence. Mirth. Desire. Amusement.

Coyness. Surprise. Pleasure. Laughter. Puzzled. Ecstasy.

MOODS AND MOMENTS: CHILDREN IN THEIR HOURS OF SMILES AND SULKS.

Our pages of Nursery "Close-Ups," by Marcus Adams, F.R.P.S., show remarkable examples of the manner in which this well-known artist of the camera can catch the fleeting expression on a child sitter's face. Mr. Marcus Adams's work is well known to "Sketch" readers, and the many admirers of his "Family Studies" will be interested by the admirable exhibition of his work which is now on view. This show

From the Portrait Studies by Marcus Adams, The Children's Studio, 43, Dover Street.

of Pictorial Photography is called "Sunshine and Shadow" —and consists of a collection of studies of children's expressions, including those shown on our pages. The show is taking place at the Royal Photographic Society of Great Britain, 38, Russell Square, W.C., and opened last week. It will continue until Feb. 25.

Exhibited at the Royal Photographic Society of Great Britain, 35, Russell Square, W.C.

greatly encouraged by his friends, that led to the formation of the Assistants' Group which became a sort of trade union with a real professional status. Adams's record in such respects is too great to include in this short biography, but he appears to have had a stimulating effect on many people, as is shown by the art groups which sought his patronage.

Once the photographic challenge ceased, Adams found a new one. Towards the end of his life, he spent many hours at his home near Wargrave, Berkshire, designing pictures made from his collection of wildflowers and grasses. From his large picture-window overlooking the Thames he completed many hundred small pastels of sunrises and sunsets. These were all signed, dated and given a time. An article in *Arts Review* in the fifties stated: 'I find it quite remarkable that a man, weaned on a black and white medium, can find such an abundance of colour nuances in the sky.'

His grandchildren, Michael, Susan and Anthony, were frequent visitors to his home at this time and provided much pleasure. Anthony recalls that 'he would sit up at his picture-window in his bedroom

Lavender Cottage, near Wargrave, Marcus Adams's home towards the end of his life.

looking over the fields, posed to capture the magnificence of the colours created as the sun slowly sank beneath the Berkshire landscape.' He went on, 'Grandpa loved his garden and spent many hours skilfully tending it. He derived great joy from all his efforts – even the plants responded to him.' Susan remembers his twinkling eyes and high-pitched laugh as he threw back his head. They remember too how he used to bang his walking stick on the floor, requesting a cup of tea.

Adams once had a dream that he paid a visit to heaven. When he arrived at the gates Saint Peter asked him a multitude of questions, and it was decided that he had insufficient experience on earth. While gaining this experience, he was told, he would greatly assist the creative powers by designing insects which he should take to heaven next time he went there. With a great deal of humour, Adams proceeded for considerable time to draw and create strange forms of animal life.

Marcus Adams's death was sudden and quite unexpected. He always appeared to be looking forward in his life, even at the age of eighty-four. He had a deep spiritual faith, and whatever he undertook he did to the highest standard, for to give anything less than his best would to him have been a sin.

On his death, his eldest grandson Michael picked hundreds of daffodils to cover his body. His granddaughter Susan, who was working at the Dover Street studio, had, a few days earlier, tried to cheer up the glass showcase by placing a large picture of Marcus Adams in the window. It was perhaps an omen for his death.

THE HON. MRS BRYAN GUINNESS WITH HER SON
JONATHAN, 1930
12³⁄₁₀ × 11¹⁄₁₀in (31.2 × 28.2cm)

Mrs Guinness was the Hon. Diana Mitford, daughter of the 2nd
Baron Redesdale. She later married Sir Oswald Mosley.

LADY BURNEY WITH HER SON CECIL, JUNE 1930
13 7⁄10 × 10⅜in (34.8 × 26.9cm)

At the time the caption to this picture ran: 'Lady Burney is the beautiful wife of Commander Sir Charles Denniston Burney, R.N., of the R.100 fame, and who is now on his return voyage across the Atlantic. The R.100 made an airship record on her outward voyage across the Atlantic to Canada, and coming home, in spite of being rather a lame duck, is sure to make good time.'

LADY LOVAT WITH THE MASTER OF LOVAT, 1920
8 × 6in (20.3 × 15.2cm)

As with many society photographers, the heyday of the Adams
studio coincided with the golden times of their sitters. The
euphoric pattern of the London season still symbolized the
affluent traces of a post-Edwardian period.

   Many people were in love with this exquisitely beautiful
woman, and when the picture was published it produced a
snowball effect on business.

THE MARQUESA DE ORIGO WITH HER SON GIANNI,
1928
6⅘ × 4⁷⁄₁₀in (17.3 × 11.9cm)

Gianni was brought to Marcus Adams's studio several times every
year for eight years. When he was eight he died, and his mother
wrote the most beautiful story about his short life, illustrating it
with Marcus Adams's photographs and many others. The
Marquesa presented Adams with a copy, which was entitled
simply 'Gianni'.

PENELOPE AND ANGELA DUDLEY-WARD, 1923
8 × 6in (20.3 × 15.2cm)

Daughters of the Right Hon. William Dudley-Ward, P.C., and Mrs Dudley-Ward. Penelope was born in 1914 and Angela in 1916. At the time Mrs Dudley-Ward was considered one of the prettiest young married women in society. William Dudley-Ward, grandson of the first Viscount Esher, was Liberal Member for Southampton from 1906 but was defeated in the election of 1922. He was formerly Vice-Chamberlain to H.M. Household and became Privy Councillor in 1922. Penelope Dudley-Ward later became an intimate friend of the Duke of Windsor.

THE INFANTAS OF SPAIN
Maria Cristina and Beatrix, daughters of Alfonso XIII
12⅗ × 11⅗in (32 × 29.5cm)

GLORIA SWANSON WITH HER BABY
7½ × 5⅗in (19 × 14.2cm)

Gloria Swanson, the American film star and actress, is the owner of Paramount Studios.

GLADYS COOPER WITH HER SON JOHN BUCKMASTER, 1921
7⁷⁄₁₀ × 5⅗in (19.5 × 14.2cm)

Marcus Adams respected his sitters, but was more intent on gaining the best pictorial effect rather than dwelling on their social status.

His staff, on the other hand, were receptive to incidents in the studio. One afternoon Robert Morley came in with his son, Sheridan, in the company of Gladys Cooper and John Buckmaster, carrying a potty and buffooning and laughing. Joan Farquharson, Marcus Adams's printer, was fascinated to see them as she was an enthusiastic follower of their respective careers.

LADY CHURSTON WITH LYDIA AND PRIMROSE, 1922
12 × 11⁷/₁₀in (30.5 × 29.7cm)

Lady Churston was formerly Denise Orme, the violinist and
comedy actress. She became the wife of the 3rd Baron in 1907,
and had two sons and four daughters. Here she is shown with the
two youngest girls, the Hon. Lydia Yarde-Buller, born in 1917,
and the Hon. Primrose Yarde-Buller, who was to marry the 7th
Earl of Cadogan in 1936.

THE KENNEDY FAMILY, 1938
11⁷/₁₀ × 9³/₅ (29.7 × 24.4cm)

Marcus Adams accepted a request to do this family portrait only
because some of the children were under sixteen.

BARBARA HUTTON WITH HER BABY, 1936
11⅕ × 9³⁄₁₀in (28.4 × 23.6cm)

PRINCESS ILYINSKY WITH HER SON PRINCE PAUL
ROMANOFF, 1930
14³⁄₁₀ × 11in (36.3 × 27.9cm)

Their Imperial Majesties were amongst many royal families from
all over the world who frequented Marcus Adams's studio.

PRINCE PAUL ROMANOFF, SON OF HIS IMPERIAL
HIGHNESS THE GRAND DUKE DIMITRI OF RUSSIA, 1929

This photograph probes the psychological intensity of the child's
mind. The subdued tonal quality of the print gives great intensity
to the eyes, reflecting the depth of thought and working of the
mind.

SUSAN, MALISE AND ANNE, 1920
The children of Mrs Guy Wilson
10⅗ × 9³⁄₁₀in (26.9 × 23.6cm)

LADY VIOLET BONHAM CARTER WITH HER SON
RAYMOND, 1935
8 × 6in (20.3 × 15.2cm)
Collection National Portrait Gallery

When Raymond was a baby Lady Violet approached Marcus
Adams with a view to his photographing mother and child in the
bedroom. Not keen to do this, Adams photographed them in the
studio but sent along his son Gilbert to carry out the bedroom
sitting.

IV
THE CHILD'S DAY

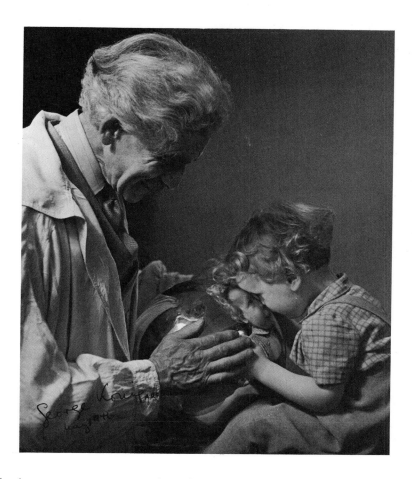

'I feel just as young as the child I am with – like Peter Pan I shall never be permitted to grow into my second childhood, because children will not allow me to get out of the first.'

To understand why Marcus Adams became internationally acclaimed as a photographer of children from 1907 until his death in 1959, it is necessary to look into the life-style of the children he photographed during these years. The domestic pattern of aristocratic families was already altering in the thirties, although the more dramatic change probably occurred around the fifties, when families who had lived in large houses and employed domestic servants and nannies were slowly forced to modify their way of life.

It must not be assumed that Marcus Adams photographed society children exclusively. To him, children were a source of inspiration whatever their background. Some three-quarters of a million plates of children, made during his lifetime, were representative of many types of childhood throughout the world. Some of his most delightful studies are those taken outside the studio routine. However, the general run of daily life of most of the sitters shown in this book displays a certain similarity. Their childhood was patterned by friendship with other families of similar social standing, developed and matured through adolescence and adulthood. Although the tendency is to think of an entirely nursery-style existence throughout the Victorian and Edwardian age, it seems that considerable changes were taking place before the twenties, and continued to do so right up to the virtual disappearance of nursery life after the sixties.

The children who feature in Marcus Adams's portraits were living in the days when fairies and elves, bunnies and goblins featured prominently, when teddy bears, golliwogs and penguins were playmates and when the rocking-horse was the anchor in many a nursery. Surprisingly, most of the people interviewed in connection with this book appear not to have been entirely nursery-bound. Parents generally saw quite a lot of their children and, with odd exceptions, children and parents were emotionally close.

In most households there was a 'magic hour' between tea and supper, the hour when children were bathed, scrubbed and changed into their fine clothes after the rigours of the afternoon walk, playtime in the park and then nursery tea. The idea was that children were seen, at least at this time of day, by their parents, without interruption and looking their best. It was the time, too, when the nanny and nursemaid could contemplate an hour's respite from repetitive demands. It is probable that, far from having this time to read the paper (which often didn't come up until Papa brought it home in the evening), Nanny was busy

'Shrimping by the Sea', c. 1912. Marcus Adams carried a camera wherever he travelled, which resulted in many photographs being taken outside the studio.

'Group of Schoolchildren', c. 1905. Here
Marcus Adams has sympathetically combined
two of his loves, children and architecture; the
latter he became deeply involved in when
illustrating a series of books on Norman
architecture for Charles Keyser.

ironing clothes and setting the nursery in order – if her charges hadn't
been made to do it first. To the children it was the hour of anticipation.
What were they going to do with Mama during the pre-cocktail period?
Sometimes they would be shown off to her friends or guests, for whom
they would sing or put on little plays. Often Mama would read aloud to
them, and sometimes, in the mêlée of the meeting hour, Papa would
come back from his club or from his work. In the big houses, of course,
he was already there, and many times in the course of discussion I have
come across fathers who tried to be as much a part of their children's life
as they could be, playing with and reading to the children. Only rarely
did I hear about that sinister, distant, autocratic gentleman so often
described.

The rudiments of reading, writing and arithmetic were taught –
usually during the morning – either by Nanny or by a governess. A
certain amount of jealousy often developed in this hierarchy, for the
nanny was very much in charge and thought herself rather superior. At
the turn of the century one nanny said to her new employer, 'I hope
you've got the silver on my dressing table?' Nannies were never meant to

clean their own stables and generally came from the same class as their employers: others began as nursemaids and were gradually promoted. Often this resulted in some royal Russian child or English aristocrat having a cockney or broad Yorkshire accent. Superior as nannies undoubtedly were to the other servants, however, the governess considered herself in a class above.

Up to the Second World War, Marcus Adams found his studio visitors easy to manage: if they got out of hand, a quick, sharp word sufficed to bring them back. This changed after the war when discipline in the home became less strict, and the outsider had a tougher task to maintain order.

The atmosphere of the nursery is well summed up by Magdalen King-Hall in *The Story of the Nursery:*

> The Nursery is a little world apart. Imagine it on a winter's evening, the red curtains drawn against the wind and the rain outside, the coal fire burning brightly behind the high fireguard, nanny sitting in her rocking chair, working through the pile of mending in the basket at her side. . . . Now and then as she rocks, she looks up and admonishes her charges, when they become too noisy or quarrelsome.

Many of those brought up in the first half of this century are happy, in retrospect, with the routine by which their secure childhood was bound. Those who emerged from the nursery discipline and programmed days, many of them distinguished men and women, were instilled with standards and morals which, whether broken or adhered to, stood them in good stead in later life.

At the time it was not thought abnormal for parents to be apart from their children. People travelled further, for longer, and communications between the Commonwealth and home were not as highly developed as they are today. One of the many reasons that Marcus Adams portraits became so popular, and in a way 'essential', was that they were conceived by him not only for the home, where photographs were displayed on the grand piano or sofa tables, but also for parents to take on their visits abroad as a constant reminder of their children.

This became especially so with the pictures of the Royal Family who, when embarking on a tour to distant parts of the Empire, invariably called for a sitting some months before the tour and every month during their absence. A number of photographs were therefore produced either for the press to mark the time of departure, or for the King and Queen, and later the Queen and Prince Philip, to have with them while they were away.

There were some children who hardly knew their fathers – one girl recalls frequently asking her nanny whether Daddy was the King or God. When he eventually did return from fighting and walked into the nursery, the child turned to the nanny and said: 'Nanny, God has just arrived.' Sunday School training was deeply rooted.

There is no doubt that strict discipline in most families did produce in the Adams sitter a certain rebelliousness, an impishness and naughtiness which time encouraged. Marcus Adams summed it up like this: 'The expression with its glimmering sparkle – flashing like a ripple on water . . . forever changing . . . glee . . . mirth . . . mischief . . . shyness . . . coyness . . . independence . . . and impudence . . . are but a few versions of the index of the little mind within.'

As can be seen from the portraits in this book, clothes played a dominant part in the children's life, right up until Adams's last sittings in 1958. The Royal Family had much to do with the way society children dressed, for as soon as pictures of the royal children were seen in the press and in the many books featuring Marcus Adams portraits of them, fashion in children's clothes followed close behind. A number of people can date their own photographs by some particular royal event, as they remember the dresses worn by the little Princesses in the twenties and thirties. Similarly, pictures of Prince Charles and Princess Anne taken by Marcus Adams in the forties and fifties reveal the year of the sitting by the style of clothes they were wearing.

The parents of Marcus Adams's sitters were advised by him on dress as follows:

Dress is of the highest importance; it can give inspiration or cause difficulties.

Dress should be part of the child, fit well, not too long and very important to see the neck-line suits the face, and kept fairly

This gold-toned portrait of Mabel Farr was taken by Marcus Adams in the Walton Adams Studio, Reading, c. 1890. May Farr, as she was later known, went on to become one of Marcus Adams's assistants in the London studio.

Marcus Adams's study of the Old Masters and their subjects led him to make many formal arrangements of the descendants of their families dressed in clothes of the period. He emulated in photography a style which had been tried and mastered by the painter of portraits. Here his portrait of Maurice and Carol Macmillan and Lord Andrew Cavendish echoes that of their forebears George Henry, Anne and William Cavendish, painted by Sir Thomas Lawrence, c. 1790 (previously attributed to John Hoppner).

low to show the neck. Not too white, or starchy-stiff, not too fussy, the outline should be simple.

Both boys' and girls' apparel was lavish, not only for parties but for everyday wear. Day dresses for girls might be of pale blue or turquoise silk, or pink organdie, with a matching bow in the hair. White cotton socks and buckle shoes would accompany them. Boys often wore the inevitable sailor-suit – a white drill blouse with blue canvas trousers. Girls' party dresses were cream net with layers of frills and slip-on shoes. Slightly earlier, in 1909, came the boys' suits of raven's wing velvet and for girls at the same period, dresses in white silk and lace. Magdalen King-Hall describes it thus:

> . . . embroidered muslin and cotton dresses with pearl beads on lace, with a brush and comb set in bone and ivory. Not only were children warmed with tailored kid gloves and smocked dresses, but so were their dollies. There was Chilprufe underwear – winter weight and summer weight – and Hip Grip shorts for playtime. Margaret Coke remembers these fabulous clothes, but rarely changing them – except for the undies.

It has been said that many of the lavish social parties were not so much for the children and parents but more for the nannies – and nannies loved them; going to tea at Buckingham Palace is a favourite reminiscence of any nanny today. Clothes for these events were extra lavish. Layers and layers of taffeta, silk and ribbon might be carefully wrapped and sent in boxes to the party, where the children had to change on arrival, though sometimes they dressed at home and walked to the parties.

One of the highlights of the children's social calendar was the preparation of the annual Charity Matinée, organized and produced by Madame Vacani. The clothes were designed with the help of a designer at Raynes, the theatrical costumiers, and made by them. In later years, when costs became too outrageous, Miss Betty Vacani delved into her own costume wardrobe and made the sketches herself. These little Vacani youngsters were captioned, in 1938, 'The Youthful Mayfair Ballerinas'. Many children had to be photographed before the event by Marcus Adams so that magazines and periodicals could publish them at the time of the Charity Matinée. Marcus Adams found the speed with which he had to assimilate an appropriate background for the costume a somewhat challenging task. He described Miss Vacani as one of the most 'ravishing' women he had ever met, full of inspiration, energy and happiness, teaching children by the hundred deportment and dancing. He co-operated with her annual matinées for many years and gave a vast amount of his time to her theatrical productions and to her publicity. The groups of children who arrived in his studio provided a tremendous amount of fun for all concerned.

PORTRAIT OF A MOTHER AND CHILD
13⁹⁄₁₀ × 11in (35.3 × 27.9cm)

Marcus Adams was always particularly intrigued with the
relationship between mother and child and sought to capture the
affection existing between them.

PORTRAIT OF A FAMILY GROUP
13 × 11³⁄₁₀in (33 × 28.7cm)

'I realized years ago a child looked at its mother so differently from looking at anyone else. This faced me with a problem; to obtain the expression I wanted. I could not possibly be mother to every child, however, I had to surmount the difficulty by love and tact and a thorough understanding of the life of a child, entering into its pleasures and difficulties, and letting every child realize I was with it in every sense of the word. And by this double sense of confidence and psychology, I began to put myself in the mother's position, then I could actually draw from the child anything I wanted to record.' Marcus Adams

THE HON. MRS GEOFFREY FRY WITH HER DAUGHTER
JENNIFER, 1922
$13\frac{3}{5} \times 10\frac{3}{10}$in (34.5 × 26.2cm)

LADY HUGH SMILEY WITH HER SON JOHN, 1935
11⅖ × 9in (28.9 × 22.8cm)

Before her marriage Lady Smiley was Nancy Beaton, one of two
sisters made famous by their brother, the photographer Cecil
Beaton. Baba was the other sister.

  'I remember the group comprising Margaret Whigham, Baba
Beaton, Nancy Beaton and Jenny Stourton being amongst the
liveliest and most devastating of my father's sitters. They used to
come to the studio draped in Cecil Beaton designed dresses made
from American cloth – the first time American cloth had been
used for costumes. They had enormous hats, studded with pearls.'
Gilbert Adams

MRS McCORQUODALE WITH HER DAUGHTER RAYNE,
1930
7⁹⁄₁₀ × 6in (20 × 15.2cm)
Collection Barbara Cartland

Mrs McCorquodale is the famous novelist Barbara Cartland. Her
daughter Rayne is married to Lord Spencer and is the stepmother
of the Princess of Wales.

MRS CHARLES SWEENY WITH HER DAUGHTER
FRANCES
$11\frac{7}{10} \times 9\frac{9}{10}$in (29.7 × 25.1cm)

MRS SPEARS WITH HER BABY, 1923
14⅖ × 11in (36.6 × 27.9cm)

The press hand-out at the time of this picture read as follows: 'Mrs Spears is the wife of Brigadier General Edward Louis Spears C.B. C.B.E. D.S.O. formerly captain and Brevet Lieutenant-Colonel 11th Hussars. He served in the European War from 1914-1918 and retired in 1920 as an Honorary Brigadier General. He is also a Commander of the Legion of Honour and has the Orders of the Star of Roumania with Swords and the White Eagle of Serbia with Swords. Mrs. Spears who is a very beautiful woman is a Chevalier of the Legion of Honour . . . .'

'Through meeting so many types of children there has formed in me an intuitive instinct which I cannot explain – the general construction of the child, its activities, the way it looks at me, the shape of head, often the thumb gives me a guide.'

Photographing royalty was nothing new to the Adams family. Walton Adams used to go regularly from his studio in Southampton to Osborne House on the Isle of Wight, to photograph Queen Victoria. Among his other sitters were members of European royal families, the Belgian in particular. He also took portraits of the Prince and Princess of Wales, and the former he photographed later as King Edward VII.

Studio royal portraiture in the nineteenth century and early twentieth century was, on the whole, dignified and unbending: the public at large received a stiff and formal glimpse of royalty. It was only when Marcus Adams created fresh, spontaneous images of the Royal Family as a group, which were published world-wide, that the public became aware of their very human aspect. Today, Marcus Adams's royal portraits may in retrospect be considered stiff and posed, so accustomed have we now become to the informality and beauty of the pictures of Lord Snowdon, Norman Parkinson and Patrick Lichfield. During the twenties, thirties, forties and even fifties, however, the public were only ready for the semi-studied compositions of the Marcus Adams portrait, and this is what they received. Thousands were treasured by humble people in homes and cottages across the land. Marcus Adams was undoubtedly the man who first brought the British Royal Family close to the people, and his achievement was pre-eminently due to the comparative informality that was permitted, whether it was at 43 Dover Street, 145 Piccadilly, Buckingham Palace or Windsor Castle. He held the Royal Warrant, and later both Marcus Adams and his son Gilbert were granted the Warrant together.

In 1926 Marcus Adams was called to Bruton Street, the home of the newly married Duke and Duchess of York, to make arrangements for a sitting to include their first-born child, Princess Elizabeth, then aged eight months. It is not absolutely clear whether, in fact, this sitting eventually took place at Dover Street or at their home, but both Queen Mary and the Duke of York were present. The little Princess was photographed by herself and with her family. It was rather difficult at one stage, Marcus Adams explained later, to focus Her Majesty Queen Mary and the little Princess simultaneously, because Queen Mary had a large frontage and the little girl was sitting some inches in front of the Queen's face. Despite these difficulties, the picture was successfully achieved (see p.107). After that initial sitting, it became a custom for the Duke and Duchess to bring their children to the studio about twice a year or, alternatively, for Marcus Adams to go to 145 Piccadilly. As with all his little sitters, Marcus called the Princesses by their Christian names. They, in turn, called him Mr Golliwog or Mr Adams. It is probable that their earliest lessons in drawing were given to them by the artist-photographer Marcus Adams.

Marcus Adams's meetings with the Royal Family were not limited merely to the sittings. Hours were often devoted to lengthy discussions about proofs, or about which pictures were to be published and which were to be retained for the family's private enjoyment. Then there were those pictures which were not to be used under any circumstances. On one such occasion Marcus Adams was discussing details with the Queen, using the floor as a table. Princess Margaret bounded into the room and saw him kneeling among the pictures, with a pencil in his hand. She was in a specially fractious mood and said that if he had a pencil, she wanted one too. Marcus Adams produced another and settled her to the task of drawing a frame for her grandfather's portrait, which meant making circles round a coin. This kept her amused for a time, but soon she began to fidget and interfere with the pictures on the carpet. She just would not keep still. At last the Queen became quite impatient with her. 'Margaret, for goodness' sake go and lose yourself!' That seemed to have the desired effect and they went on working. Suddenly the Queen looked at Marcus Adams and he at her. 'Where's Margaret?' Then they saw a pair of eyes, with the wickedest, most mischievous look in them, peering over the edge of a big leather waste-paper basket in which the Princess had 'lost' herself. She screamed with delight, rocked the basket till it toppled over and then rolled yards across the floor inside it.

Princess Elizabeth in contrast was a very motherly type of child. After seeing one of the most beautiful photographs of herself that Marcus Adams took in his thirty years of royal photography (see p.120) she was determined to see her sister Margaret portrayed in the same pose. So, when Margaret reached the same age, the picture was arranged by Lillibet and, indeed, it proved to be one of the loveliest of Princess Margaret.

Not only did these royal sittings create a familiar image of the Royal Family all over the world, but they brought a considerable amount of work and business to the studio.

One of the most widely published and remarkable photographs of the King and Queen and two Princesses is that taken in the doorway of one of the rooms at Buckingham Palace. Marcus Adams once remarked to his son Gilbert, 'Oh dear, what am I going to use for background at the Palace?' and was rather deflated when Gilbert turned to him and replied: 'What do you mean, Pops, with all those wonderful backgrounds and rooms?' This particular sitting had been arranged in order to get a profile of Princess Elizabeth for a stamp to be issued in Newfoundland. (Many stamps were issued of all members of the Royal Family from pictures taken by Marcus Adams.) On this occasion there was much merriment and Gilbert, who was assisting, kept on saying 'Retake!' as the Princess burst into helpless giggles. For the group picture, the King suggested that the dog, Dukie, should be included, but Dukie had other ideas so Marcus Adams pulled a biscuit out of his pocket, knelt down

Photographs taken by Marcus Adams of himself taking photographs of the Duchess of York and Princess Elizabeth and the Duke of Kent with Prince Edward. Visible are his etched marks indicating how the final prints should be proportioned.

*Portrait of the Duchess of York and Princess Elizabeth, December
1926. This was the first sitting Marcus Adams had with Queen
Mary, the Duke and Duchess of York and Princess Elizabeth,
when the little Princess was eight months old.*

There were difficulties with the making of this picture, as Gilbert Adams described: 'Because it was a large group it had to be made with a very wide aperture and although we always imported additional light there was a technical problem. The chandeliers had gone out of focus and caused a tremendous lot of blobbing of lights and spots. In order to get the whole room in focus, we had another film made from exactly the same position. The two negatives were ultimately bound up together with the original background having been bleached out. This was a tricky operation; one fraction of a second could have ruined the original negative, because of using a chemical like ferrocyanide to do the bleaching. If you once let it slip across the part you want you have ruined it. It took a day to do the job. Reproductions of this picture ran into millions.'

and placed it on the King's shoe. When asked where it came from, Marcus Adams said, 'It's quite all right, Sir, it came from Buckingham Palace.' It had been saved from his morning coffee. When the dog came over to fetch the biscuit, it remained still for a fraction of a second, so Marcus Adams obtained his picture.

This stage of royal photography ceased for Adams soon after the outbreak of the Second World War. Princess Elizabeth was then growing up, though the children of the Princes of Kent and Gloucester continued to be photographed by him.

At the end of the war, however, Princess Elizabeth was to marry Prince Philip, and, with the arrival of Prince Charles, there were more royal commissions for Marcus Adams. The excitement of the first sitting with the little Prince is vividly described by Sylvia Bennett, Marcus Adams's assistant, in a diary entry for 26 October 1949.

Today has been very special. At about 2.45 this afternoon I was introduced by Mr Adams to Princess Elizabeth in the capacity

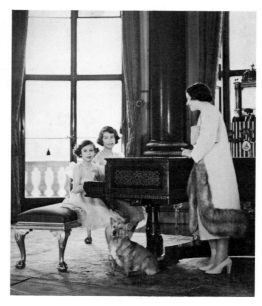

This informal shot of Her Majesty The Queen with the two Princesses at Buckingham Palace was taken in 1938 or 1939 by Gilbert Adams who, acting as Marcus Adams's assistant at the time, happened to have his Rolleiflex camera handy.

of his assistant. This was the culmination of a long-awaited hope. The realization of it was clinched last Wednesday when Princess Elizabeth's lady-in-waiting arranged an appointment with Mr Adams for the taking of Prince Charles with his mother. Great was the cleaning and polishing that followed and today the studio looked perfect with Mr Park's beautiful chrysanthemums as the finishing touch.

Excitement reached fever pitch when at last the Princess arrived at 2.30 with Nurse Lightbody and the baby. The sitting went off perfectly. Prince Charles laughed and smiled. Princess Elizabeth smiled and laughed and chatted to everyone, including me, so naturally. She is really charming. The time passed all too quickly, despite the fact that we were in the studio over an hour and a half. Miss Newcombe was very thrilled when she was given Prince Charles to hold while the Nurse collected all her belongings. I amused him with a silver rattle while he waited. He chuckled and held on to my finger. Both Mr Vintner and I received another handshake as she left. A very emotional Mr Adams kissed me in the studio when all was over, and I thanked him for the honour I had received at being present at such an auspicious occasion. He has now taken three generations of the Royal Family.

Now the fun really starts. Our pictures will be used for the Prince's birthday. Life's going to be hectic. . . .

The diary continues on 13 November:

Our pictures of the Princess and her baby came out in all the papers today. In these last few days all of 43 have been working on and sending out over a thousand prints. I have never known such a commotion from Fleet Street, directed at us. To start this week we have to get over three hundred by Tuesday for press release. I don't know when it will lessen. In America they would have the same positions in their Sunday papers. They were radioed out there.

Once Princess Anne was born and came to be photographed regularly with her brother, the fun and games began all over again. Prince Charles used to scream with laughter when, on looking through the lens, he saw his sister facing him upside down. Wanting her to experience this phenomenon too, he told her to stand behind the camera and then jumped into position himself, trying to stand on his head so Princess Anne would see him the right way up. Unfortunately he couldn't quite make it.

Marcus Adams's thirty years as a royal photographer spanned four generations of Royals, from George V and Queen Mary to Princess Anne. The charming spontaneous photographs of Prince Charles and Princess Anne in the 1950s prove that, even in his eighties, Adams was still fresh and dynamically committed to instilling the magic into his hour's studio playtime. It was unfortunate that his death robbed him of the chance of photographing the Queen's other children, Prince Edward and Prince Andrew, thus completing the era as photographer royal.

Her Majesty The Queen with Prince Charles and Princess Anne, 1951.

HER MAJESTY QUEEN MARY WITH PRINCESS
ELIZABETH, 1927
14 × 10⅘ (35.6 × 27.4cm)

THE DUCHESS OF YORK WITH PRINCESS ELIZABETH,
JULY 1928
11⅘ × 10½in (30 × 26.7cm)

Whoever would refuse Royalty! Marcus Adams did just that, at the beginning of his London career, in 1920. Why? His rule was that he did not photograph anyone over the age of sixteen. So when the Countess of Strathmore endeavoured to persuade him to photograph her daughter, Lady Elizabeth Bowes Lyon, he asked how old she was, and was told that she was about twenty. 'Well, I'm awfully sorry, I must decline,' said Adams. 'However, on the other hand, if she marries and has children then I should be delighted to photograph her with her children.'

THE DUKE OF YORK WITH PRINCESS ELIZABETH, JULY 1929
13$\frac{1}{10}$ × 10$\frac{1}{2}$in (33.3 × 26.7cm)

The royal children were often accompanied to the studio by the
Duke, who hated to miss out on the fun and games.

PRINCESS ELIZABETH
8¹⁄₁₀ × 6¹⁄₅in (20.6 × 15.7cm)

Photographs taken between December 1926 and June 1927 when Princess Elizabeth was brought to Marcus Adams's studio by Queen Mary and Nurse Knight (see also p. 107). The monthly photographs were then sent out to her parents, who were on an extended tour of Australia and New Zealand.

PRINCESS ELIZABETH, DECEMBER 1926
14 × 10⅘in (35.6 × 27.4cm)

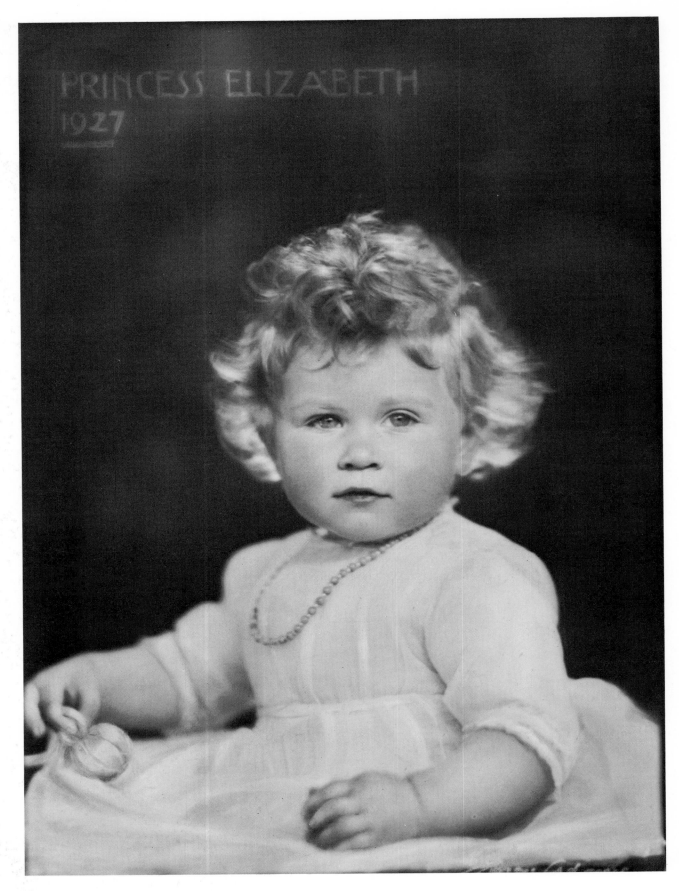

PRINCESS ELIZABETH, JUNE 1927
14¹⁄₁₀ × 10²⁄₅in (35.8 × 26.4cm)

This was the first photograph of the Princess taken after the Duke
and Duchess of York returned from their tour of Australia and
New Zealand.

PRINCESS MARGARET ROSE AGED TWO, 1932
13³⁄₁₀ × 10³⁄₁₀in (33.8 × 26.2cm)

A delightfully happy and radiant portrait of the young Princess.

THE DUCHESS OF YORK PROUDLY ENJOYING THE
COMPANY OF HER TWO YOUNG DAUGHTERS, 1936
9⅗ × 7⁷⁄₁₀in (24.4 × 19.5cm)

This delightful study was taken while The Queen Mother was still
Duchess of York and shortly before she was to take on the
responsibilities of Queen as a result of the abdication by her
brother-in-law, the Duke of Windsor.

PRINCESS ELIZABETH, NOVEMBER 1934
13⁹⁄₁₀ × 11in (35.3 × 27.9cm)

During one of the royal sittings, at the request of the Duke of York, Gilbert Adams made a movie film of Princess Elizabeth. A ball was thrown against the wall to keep the Princess's expression alert. Then half a dozen balls were thrown in all directions, until towards the end of film-making one ball came towards the camera, effectively closing the film.

PRINCESS ELIZABETH AND PRINCESS MARGARET,
NOVEMBER 1934
13 × 10in (33 × 25.4cm)

PRINCESS ELIZABETH AND PRINCESS MARGARET,
FEBRUARY 1939
13⁹⁄₁₀ × 10⅘in (35.3 × 27.4cm)

PRINCESS ELIZABETH AND PRINCESS MARGARET,
DECEMBER 1938
13½ × 9⅗in (34.3 × 24.4cm)

Joan Farquharson recalls that she was so excited to see the Royals
on one occasion that she along with another assistant crept down
to the concrete cupboard where the royal negatives and lenses
were kept under the stairs. When the King and Queen were on the
verge of departing into Dover Street, Adams stopped to say
something. The King took some time to reply, during which time
the girls under the stairs were shaking with giggles but unable to
get out for fear of being seen.

PRINCESS ELIZABETH AGED THIRTEEN, 1938
11⅖ × 7⅘in (28.9 × 19.8cm)

As a young child Princess Elizabeth conceived many games, both
when Marcus Adams visited her home and when she came to the
studio. On one occasion Lillibet, as she was called by her
photographer, rushed out to him, declaring: 'You have been
mortally wounded at Hyde Park Corner – lie down!' Such was her
will and intention that Marcus Adams did just that. 'Now you are
dead,' she continued, 'and you must wait until the ambulance
comes.' Luckily before long the imaginary ambulance arrived, and
with it the rest of the family.

PRINCESS ELIZABETH AND PRINCESS MARGARET, 1938
7⅘ × 5⅘in (19.8 × 14.7cm)

Here the two Princesses are attempting to solve a giant jigsaw puzzle at Windsor Castle.

HER MAJESTY THE QUEEN AND THE TWO PRINCESSES, 1941
8¹⁄₁₀ × 5½in (20.6 × 14cm)
Photographed with their two favourite corgis at Windsor Castle.

PRINCESS ELIZABETH, JULY 1928
14¹⁄₁₀ × 11³⁄₁₀in (35.8 × 28.7cm)

Surely one of the most enchanting child photographs of the
century. The Princess herself was so pleased with this picture that
she asked Marcus Adams whether he would take a similar one
of her sister when she reached the same age.

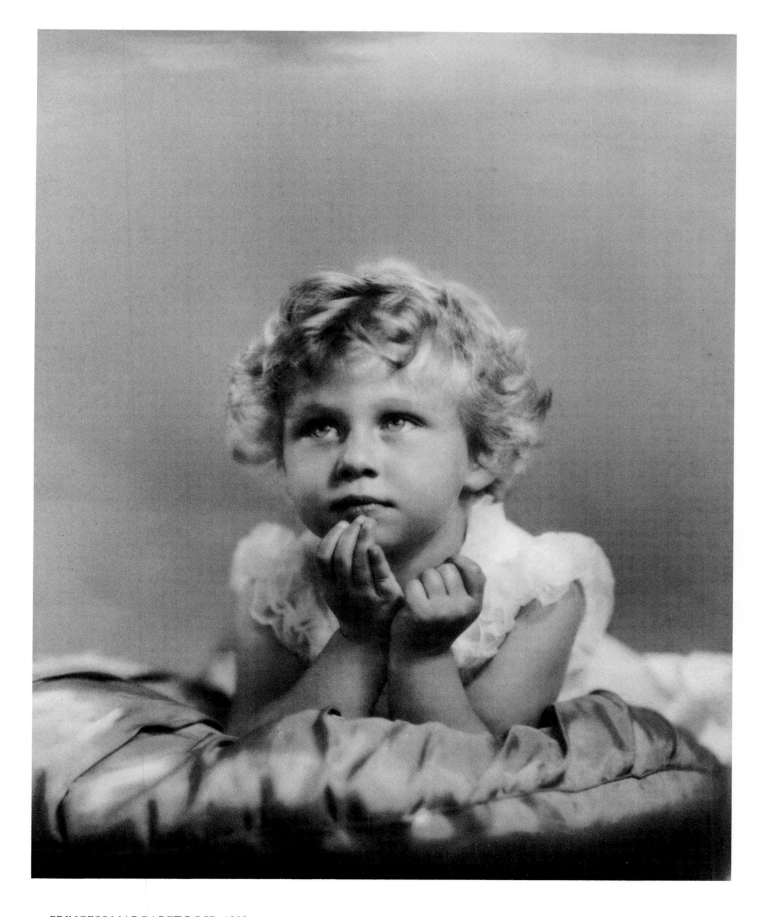

PRINCESS MARGARET ROSE, 1933
13⅘ × 10⅗ (35 × 26.9cm)

Marcus Adams succeeded in recapturing the similar attitude and
exquisite expression with Princess Margaret.

PRINCESS ELIZABETH, 1929
6⅕ × 8in (15.7 × 20.3cm)

The young Princess was full of lively pranks. On one occasion when a sitting had been organized at 145 Piccadilly, Marcus Adams on arriving heard a piercing shriek and as the door opened saw a little white frock disappearing into the house. A few moments later Princess Elizabeth came demurely into the room. 'Good morning Mr Adams,' she said as she picked up the telephone and began talking to Australia. For several moments she carried on a conversation with the imaginary Australian and then added, 'I expect you would like to speak to Marcus Adams. Yes, he is here, I'll call him.' She turned to Adams, handed him the receiver and said, 'Australia would like to have a word with you.'

PRINCESS ANNE, JULY 1954
10%⁄₁₀ × 9in (27.7 × 22.9cm)

The dress worn here by the Princess is similar in style and fabric to that worn by her mother for a sitting with Marcus Adams in 1929 (opposite page).

PRINCESS ANNE, 1954
11⅘ × 8⅘in (30 × 22.4cm)

PORTRAIT OF PRINCESS ANNE, 1954
14½ × 11½in (36.8 × 29.2cm)

HER MAJESTY THE QUEEN WITH PRINCESS ANNE, 1954
14 × 10⅗in (35.6 × 26.9cm)

James Vintner and Sylvia Bennett, Marcus Adams's studio
assistants, were both impressed by the beauty and freshness of Her
Majesty's complexion when she came to be photographed.

PRINCE CHARLES AGED THREE, JULY 1951
14 × 10⅘in (35.6 × 27.4cm)

The Prince is clearly playing to the photographer here.

PRINCESS ELIZABETH WITH PRINCE CHARLES, 1949
14³⁄₁₀ × 11¹⁄₅in (36.3 × 28.4cm)
(Reproduced by kind permission of The Camera Club)

INDEX